Mature R
Instruction

Lesson Plans Level 2

Piper
Books

Contents

Introduction

"Teaching students the basic letter-sound combinations gives them access to sounding out approximately 84% of the words in English print." – Wiley Bevans, International Literacy Association

It's a priceless gift to be able to teach a student to read accurately and fluently. These lessons are here to give you complete confidence in your ability to deliver that learning. Teacher training all too often omits a comprehensive understanding of "how reading works" – the logic underpinning written language, and the laser-like precision and copious amounts of practice required for weaker students. Phonics is simply a method of teaching people to read by correlating sounds with symbols in an alphabetic writing system. Overwhelming scientific evidence suggests that this is the most effective way of teaching reading: "*helpful for all children, harmful for none, and crucial for some.*"[1] Similarly, the evidence is clear that "*Putting to-be-learned material in a story format improves learning outcome.*"[2]

The eighty-one Mature Reading Instruction (MRI) stories, plays and poems are designed for secondary school students and adults with weak reading skills. The first two (of five) Levels are also suitable for upper-primary pupils. They address:

[1] Pamela Snow, 'The Snow Report'.
[2] Daniel Willingham, Professor of Psychology, University of Virginia.

- Inadequate Decoding
- Poor Comprehension
- Limited Vocabulary
- Lack of Fluency
- Guessing Strategies
- Knowledge Deficit
- Weak Memory
- Inaccurate Spelling

Inadequate Decoding. Struggling readers have often been denied straightforward, consistent Synthetic Phonics instruction. The five MRI Levels gradually introduce and thoroughly practice each new letter(s)/sound pair. The 95,000-wordcount provides the plentiful amounts of varied repetition and overlearning necessary for decoding to become automatic.

Poor Comprehension. Ensuring that a student's comprehension abilities keep pace with their improving decoding skills is vital. MRI's thought-provoking tales from around the world, and the accompanying Comprehension Questions, offer ample opportunities for discussion and exploration.

Limited Vocabulary. *"Vocabulary forms a relentless divide between children who succeed and those who do not"*.[3] MRI's expressive prose and accompanying Vocabulary Questions dramatically reduce this deficit.

Lack of Fluency. *"Fluency refers to the reader's ability to develop*

[3] Susan B. Neuman, *All About Words.*

control over surface-level text processing so that he or she can focus on understanding the deeper levels of meaning embedded in the text".[4] Reading and rereading the MRI tales supports the transition from painful effort to expressive ease. The MRI Tutor Guide also provides extensive Timed Word Reading for each Level.

Guessing Strategies. Damaging strategies such as guessing and multi-cueing are a common feature amongst those who lack secure decoding skills. For the student who does not understand "how reading works" the temptation to use confusing mixed methods, aka "guessing" and 3-cueing, can be irresistible. With the simple instruction to *"Say the sounds and read the word"* MRI provides a clear focus on decoding for reading, and encoding for spelling.

Knowledge Deficit. From Africa's mischievous spider demi-god to the Norse World-Tree, from the Aborigine Rainbow Snake to the Indian Princess who defies Death, MRI provides a wealth of cultural capital from around the world. Condensed versions of *Beowulf, Wuthering Heights, Pride and Prejudice, Frankenstein* and five Shakespeare plays also offer a gateway into the riches of the English literary canon.

Weak Memory. *"Your memory is not a product of what you want to remember or what you try to remember; it's a product of what you think about"*.[5] Securing the Alphabetic Code in long-term memory is greatly enhanced by the thought-provoking nature of the MRI tales and accompanying Discussion Questions.

Inaccurate Spelling. Short dictations, taken from the stories, are recommended for most lessons. It soon becomes clear which students require more intensive spelling practice. The

[4] Tim Rasinski, 'Creating Fluent Readers'.
[5] Jo Facer, *Simplicity Rules.*

Level 2 Word Lists contain most Advanced Code and multi-syllable words; use these for short one-to-one or small group dictation sessions. Single-word dictation has many advantages for struggling readers: it carries less cognitive load, and focuses on sounding-through-the-word encoding, allowing additional time for handwriting development and practice.

The **Mature Reading Instruction Tutor Guide** offers Initial and Mastery Assessments, Background Notes, Sequence of Phoneme/Graphemes, Tutor Record Sheets, Timed Word Fluency Reading, Dictation/Copying exercises and additional advice in the Troubleshooting section.

Pre-Lesson

Assess each student individually with the Sound Check (MRI Level 2 p4). Point at each letter in turn, correct errors immediately, and if necessary run through the test again.

Use the Initial Assessment (MRI Tutor Guide p16-19; also available at www.piperbooks.co.uk/mri-free-resources) and fill in the graph for each student. Initial and Mastery Assessments are essential tools for tracking progress.

Materials

For the teacher:
MRI Level 2, large whiteboard or visualizer, and an A4 folder on each student, clearly labelled with their name, year group, class and chronological age at the start of the programme.

For the student:

MRI Level 2, mini-whiteboard, marker and wiper, exercise book, pen and pointer. The pointer is optional; a pencil/finger is a viable alternative. The students' exercise books should be clearly labelled with name, class and year group, if applicable.

Teaching Points

- **If a lesson is overrunning:** It is essential to ensure that every student's phonics knowledge is secure before moving on. If necessary, focus on reading and vocabulary development rather than rushing to cover all suggested activities.
- **If a lesson is underrunning:** Allow ten minutes for silent reading. Ask students to use their finger/pointer; listen to their "inner voice"; and concentrate on the language and meaning of the story. Circulate at this stage, monitoring how each student approaches their reading and making a note of anyone who struggles before inviting thoughts on the story. Introduce additional spelling, timed word reading, syllable chunking, or graphic sequencing.
- Assure students at the start that their literacy difficulties are not their fault, and can be overcome by acquiring the simple habit of accurate decoding, and by eradicating damaging habits like guessing.
- Error correction: when a student makes a mistake, correct immediately. When a student hesitates, prompt "the sound here is '___'" after three seconds.
- Quality of feedback after each class reading of a passage is vital. Do not rush this stage. Model expressive reading once more, if necessary.

- Always be alert for any students who fall behind; they have had years of shame and practice in covering up what they perceive as their failure. It is much more important that no student is left behind than that the programme is completed within a particular timescale. If there is no opportunity for additional tutoring, and a teaching assistant is unavailable, a weaker student might be paired with a mature reader for extra practice in rereading, copying, dictation, phoneme deletion and/or phoneme substitution.
- Make it clear that students are to answer any question – written or oral – with a full sentence.
- When reading in unison with students, Ⓣ should remind them to "*Say the sounds and read the word*" and pace their own reading accordingly.
- When each line/paragraph of a story is being read in turn by an individual student and cold calling is not being employed, decide the best way of organising the students (front-to-back-row, clockwise, alphabetical name order, etc). Thoroughly drill them in this protocol before embarking on the lessons.
- Decide on a simple word/gesture to indicate when students should simultaneously hold up their "show me" whiteboards during a multiple-choice exercise.
- A sample answer *[in italics and square brackets]* is provided for the T's convenience after each question.

Reading "*The strategy of repeated reading is a well-practised method to develop fluency, particularly if the rereading is undertaken after a good reader role model*".[6] The instructions on

[6] Alex Quigley, *Closing the Reading Gap.*

how to divide up the repeated reading of a story are adaptive. Some teachers take the opportunity during their initial modelling of a story to "*concisely explain vocabulary, ask questions, or offer clarifications, during the act of reading*".[7] If time is limited, teacher modelling can be reduced to the more difficult passages rather than the whole story. If time is very limited, shorter stories can be omitted, *provided any new letter(s)/sound pairs are clearly introduced and thoroughly practiced.* If students are struggling with the cold call reading, temporarily replace this step with another reading in unison, minus the T.

Introduction of Grapheme/Phonemes **T** should write each new spelling/sound on the board, leaving them up for the whole lesson and clearly introducing both the sound and word examples. Make it clear that backslashes (/ /) indicate *sounds* and single speech marks (' ') indicate *letters.*

Comprehension – Oral Questions "*Promoting high-quality questioning in the classroom may just prove the most important way to promote the strategic thinking that improves our pupils' reading. By promoting, structuring and modelling questions relentlessly, and integrating them into classroom reading routines, we help pupils at every stage... before, during and after their reading.*"[8]

Wait for responses from students. There will be silence at first. Expect this. If no replies, direct students to the appropriate paragraph for them to silently reread. Encourage well-explained answers. The ability to articulate a clear and accurate oral response is essential for comprehension and not to be rushed. Model the initial feedback if necessary. Offer positive reinforcement when a student ventures a response. If it's

7 Ibid.

8 Ibid.

wrong, say "Good try, Lizzie, but look again and see what the character intends..." If the answer is correct, say: "Excellent Mohammed, that is exactly right. Does everyone see how that is the right answer?" Model again where there are obvious issues in student understanding.

For the most part, allow students to put their hands up but keep a sharp eye out for the quieter ones and cold call when necessary to ensure that everyone engages with the questions and has a good grasp of the material. Many students have had several years of practice in hiding the "shame" of their illiteracy from teachers. Be sensitive to their fear of public humiliation but do not allow them to slip through the net once more.

Comprehension – Oral Discussion Encourage students to answer the questions carefully. Short/weak answers should be developed by T modelling more complex thought processes and attention to textual detail for how we show further/deeper understanding.

Often students lose sight of the discussion question; if that happens, direct them back to it. If they *are* focusing on the discussion question then give positive reinforcement. A lot of important cognitive activity is happening here.

Vocabulary – Oral "*You need to drill the class to use their mini-whiteboards to simultaneously perform the 'show me' action in a crisp, prompt manner. Crucially, you need students to hold up the boards long enough for you to engage with their responses.*"[9]

Decoding 'ee', sound /ee/ and 'e', sound /ee/ are Advanced Code; other letters that double-up (ff, ll, ss) are treated as Basic Code. Other common pronunciations – e.g. 's' as /z/ (slug<u>s</u>), 'f'

[9] Adapted from Sherrington, T., 'Ten teaching techniques to practise – deliberately', Teacherhead.

as /v/ (of) are also left for students to "tweak" for themselves rather than being officially introduced.

Writing Although writing is a powerful cognitive reinforcement of learning, MRI uses writing sparingly in the earlier Levels in order to concentrate on decoding, fluency and comprehension. Schools have their own handwriting policy, which should be followed.

Spelling Encourage students to concentrate on the Advanced Code part of a word – see **Appendix D**.

Please do not hesitate to contact Piper Books on enquires@piperbooks.co.uk with any queries or feedback.

Level 2
Lesson Plans

Week 1 Lesson 1: I am Cat: Playing With the Rat

Sound Check

T: copy onto whiteboard/visualizer the right-hand column of Mature Reading Instruction Level 2 p5. Ask students to read out each word in unison as you point to it. For those who have just completed MRI Level 1, this will serve as a reminder of the many new grapheme-phoneme Advanced Code correspondences they have learnt. For those able to skip Level 1 and start here, it will confirm whether the Advanced Code knowledge they require is secure.

Dictation

T dictates the following words, assuring students that some of them aren't real words they will ever have heard of – they are made-up but anyone with a secure knowledge of the Basic Alphabetic Code will be able to work out how to spell them:
elm, det, dragon, imp, yis, job, prin, grug, jacket

Ⓣ: "What do you think the point of including made-up words was?"
[There are two vital strands to reading: decoding the text and comprehending it. (See **Appendix A.**) *It is important that decoding – proceeding sound-by-sound through each word – is both accurate and practiced enough to become automatic.]*

Phoneme Breakdown

Ⓣ: write on the whiteboard the fifteen words in the left-hand column below. For the first word, cold call a student to tell you "How many sounds? Say each sound." Read the rest of the words aloud, pausing for students to write the number of sounds on their whiteboards and to hold them up. (See **Vocabulary – Oral** on p12 for whiteboard protocol.) Cold call one student per word to give the actual sounds. (Answers in right-hand column. Bold font shows two or more letters for one sound.)

Go over and model any words that caused confusion.

sheep	*[3*	***sh ee*** *p]*
brown	*[4*	*b r* ***ow*** *n]*
her	*[2*	*h* ***er****]*
sheet	*[3*	***sh ee*** *t]*
slipper	*[5*	*s l i* ***pp er****]*
crown	*[4*	*c r* ***ow*** *n]*
north	*[3*	*n* ***or th****]*
silent	*[6*	*s i l e n t]*
stay	*[3*	*s t* ***ay****]*

think	*[4*	***th** i n k]*
robber	*[4*	*r o **bb er**]*
fort	*[3*	*f **or** t]*
okay	*[3*	*o k **ay**]*
when	*[3*	***wh** e n]*
shout	*[3*	***sh ou** t]*

Phoneme Deletion

T: write the left-hand column below on the board. Then sound out the first word – /b/ /l/ /e/ /d/ – and say "Bled without the /b/ sound is /l/ /e/ /d/ – led. On your whiteboards, write down the word for 'clash' without the /c/ sound." After a few seconds, ask students to simultaneously hold up their whiteboards and say the new word. Then continue through the list, with students wiping the boards between each word. Check all responses quickly and provide immediate feedback when errors occur.

bled	*delete the /b/*	*[led]*
clash	*delete the /c/*	*[lash]*
feel	*delete the /l/*	*[fee]*
feel	*delete the /f/*	*[eel]*
land	*delete the /n/*	*[lad]*
snag	*delete the /s/*	*[nag]*
smash	*delete the /m/*	*[sash]*

Contractions & Suffixes

T: "A *contraction* is a shortened form of a word that leaves out certain letters or sounds. In most contractions, an apostrophe represents the missing letters." On the whiteboard, write the phrases below, modelling the first one ("I am" – "I…m") and cold call students to provide the contracted versions:

I am

She is

Can not

You will

That is

T: "A *suffix* is a letter or group of letters which is added to the end of a word which changes its meaning or grammatical function. The suffix in the poem we are about to read is 'ing'." Ask each student to suggest a word that can have the suffix "ing" added to it.

Reading

i. T reads Poem 1 with prosody.
ii. Students quietly read the poem in unison with T, placing pointer or finger under each word.
iii. T cold calls a student for each verse/couple of lines (depending on student numbers) until passage is completed.
iv. T provides feedback as necessary.

Memorization

T: ask students to choose their favourite verse (not the last two verses!) and spend five minutes learning it off by heart before pairing up to recite to each other.

Dictation

 (See **Dictation** in **Appendix D**, p136)

Then I biff him and bash him.

A sleek and fat black rat.

I let my rat go so he thinks that he's free.

Why is his flesh so crisp?

Week 1 Lesson 2: The Frogs Demand a King

Background Knowledge

If students have completed Level 1, ask what they can remember about Aesop's Fables. If Level 1 has been skipped, explain that a fable is a short story involving talking animals and illustrating a moral lesson. Aesop's fables have endured for over two and a half thousand years, even though "he" may well be a group of people rather than an individual.

Introducing

/ng/ 'ng'

Reading

i. Ⓣ reads circa two minutes of Story 1 with prosody.
ii. Students quietly read the story in unison with T, placing pointer or finger under each word.
iii. Students read a sentence/paragraph each until story is completed, in whichever order the T established at the beginning (see p10), until story is completed.
iv. T provides feedback as necessary.

Vocabulary – Oral

Ⓣ writes "ignorant" on the board, reads it aloud and then reads the whole sentence ("We are all a bit ignorant"). T then reads aloud the three different options and asks students to write down the answer (a. b. or c.) on their show-me whiteboards. T signals students to hold up their answers for checking before students wipe their boards and T moves on to the next sentence. (NB: correct answer is the square-bracketed, italicised one.) Reveal the correct responses at the end of the exercise and if several students gave a wrong answer, discuss the problem word in the original and several other contexts.

We are all a bit ignorant. **Ignorant** – is it:
a. talented
[b. uninformed]
c. enthusiastic

It springs back up to bob around. **Bob** – is it:
a. look
b. zoom
[c. bounce]

Sorcoz... opens his big gob. **Gob** – is it:

a. hands
b. house
[c. mouth]

All the praying... begins afresh. **Afresh** – is it:

[a. anew]
b. angrily
c. cheerfully

A Stork who... prowls. **Prowl** – is it:

a. scowl
b. growl
[c. skulk]

Phoneme Substitution

Where **Phoneme Deletion** involves removing a sound, **Phoneme Substitution** involves replacing one sound with another. **T**: write the left-hand column below on the board. Say the first word and then say "What word do we have if we change the /m/ in 'must' to /j/? On your whiteboards, write down the new word." After several seconds, ask students to simultaneously hold up their whiteboards and say the new word. Then continue through the list, with students wiping the boards between each word.

must	*/m/ to /j/*	*[just]*
stiff	*/i/ to /u/*	*[stuff]*
shed	*/sh/ to /r/*	*[red]*
pit	*/t/ to /p/*	*[pip]*
pink	*/i/ to /u/*	*[punk]*
cup	*/p/ to /t/*	*[cut]*

Characterization

T: pair up students and give them ten minutes to look through the story, finding as many words as possible associated with the frogs and the kings. Ask them to write the words down as they go along, in the correct column – having created three columns entitled *Frogs King Log King Stork*. Make it clear excellent spelling and handwriting are more important than the number of words achieved.

*[**Frogs***	***King Log***	***King Stork***
plump	*splash*	*gulps*
gulps	*brown*	*snaps*
hop	*bobs*	*slaps*
jump	*big*	*pink*
swim	*lump*	*scowls*
splash		*prowls*
free		*growls*
prays		*big*
begs		*fat*
nags		*grabs*
sobs		*pecks*
ignorant		*nips*
huffs		*clack*
puffs		*bad]*
smug		
stamps		
green		
howl		
bleed		
dash		
lay		

Recall Quiz

Ensure that students have closed their books.

Name one of the frogs.
[p18-19 Sorcoz, Jazz, Thaz, Pigwig, Zack, Frank. Take answers from six students.]

Name both of the kings.
[p16, p18 Log and Stork.]

What have the frogs got against King Log?
[p17 He is completely useless.]

What have the frogs got against King Stork?
[p18 He viciously attacks them.]

Expressions

Ⓣ: introduce the following sayings and discuss students' understanding of them:

Let sleeping dogs lie.

Be careful what you wish for.

If it ain't broke don't fix it.

Comprehension – Oral Discussion

Why do some of the frogs want a king? Why don't some of the frogs want a king? *Is* this more of a warning against monarchies or against gods? Why would the gods want to punish them? Can you think of any reasons a lot of people prefer to live in a monarchy?

Week 1 Lesson 3: She Who Has Lots of Pals…

Reading

i. **T** reads Story 2 with prosody.
ii. Students quietly read the story in unison with T, placing pointer or finger under each word.
iii. Each student reads a sentence/paragraph each until story is completed.
iv. T provides feedback as necessary.

Vocabulary – Oral

(See p12 for instructions.)

The hounds… panting and braying behind her. **Bray** – is it:
a. a whisper
[b. a loud harsh noise]
c. a miaow

Gang of slavering dogs. **Slavering** – is it:
a. sleepy
[b. drooling]
c. angry

She just scampers on. **Scampers** – is it:
[a. scurries]
b. carries
c. wanders

"Another day, perhaps," blusters the bull. **Blusters** – is it:

a. cries

[b. bluffs]

c. hisses

Her pal, the Ram. **Ram** – is it:

[a. a male sheep]

b. a female sheep

c. an old male horse

Her pal, the Colt. **Colt** – is it:

a. a male sheep

b. a young female horse

[c. a young male horse]

Sentence Reworking

T: write the following sentence on the whiteboard, reading it aloud: "When she spots the ten big hounds, bounding and panting and braying behind her, she controls her panic and sprints up to her pal, the Steed." Repeat the first segment ("When she spots the ten big hounds") and ask if anyone can rephrase this. Do the same for the three subsequent segments, modelling if necessary.
[As soon as Rabbit sees the ten huge dogs leaping and puffing and howling on her heels, she manages to keep calm and runs to her friend the horse.]

Repeat for:

"Rabbit snorts in disgust, but cannot stop to reprimand him. She just scampers on to her pal, the Bull."
[Rabbit sneers in contempt, but has no time to reproach him. She just races on to find her friend the Bull.]

"'That pathetic Steed will not lend me a hand!' she pants."
['That miserable horse refuses to help me!' she puffs.]

Phoneme Substitution

(See p21 for instructions.)

ring	*/ng/ to /d/*	*[rid]*
town	*/ow/ to /e/*	*[ten]*
duck	*/ck/ to /ll/*	*[dull]*
task	*/t/ to /c/*	*[cask]*
snap	*/n/ to /l/*	*[slap]*
bitter	*/i/ to /e/*	*[better]*

Syllable Chunking

rabb it, bigg er, fall en, black ness, tempt ing, con trol, mast er, dis gust, butt er cup, ig nor ant, Sor coz

T: ask students to draw three horizonal lines on their whiteboards. Model "*rabb it*" with a pause between the two syllables and an exaggerated jaw-drop with a hand under the chin to show that each syllable contains a vowel sound. Dictate the next word – "*bigg er*" – and ask students to write one syllable on each line, holding up whiteboards when requested and erasing each word before moving on to the next. Promptly correct any errors that arise, but please assure students that there is some leeway for different interpretations – e.g. *Sorc oz* is fine, *disg ust* isn't.

Dictation

Rabbit snorts in disgust.

The hot panting of the hounds at her heels.

"The horror! The horror!" weeps the Colt.

Comprehension – Oral Questions

How would you describe Rabbit?
[Vain, arrogant, optimistic, brave, persistent, smug.]

How would you describe the hounds?
[Big, noisy, drooling, terrifying, vicious, murderous.]

Comprehension – Oral Discussion

She who has lots of pals… has no pals at all. Do you think this is true? How does it apply to your own life? What is your definition of "friend"?

Silent Reading

Ten to fifteen minutes of silently reading *She Who Has Lots of Pals…* Ask students to listen to their "inner voice" and to the language and meaning of the story, whilst still using their finger/pointer. Circulate at this stage, monitoring how each student is approaching their reading and making a note of anyone who struggles. Ask for any student thoughts on the story.

Week 1 Lesson 4: The Fox and the Robin, I am Cat: Playing in the Tree & Keep the Cat

The Fox and the Robin

Reading

i. Ⓣ reads first paragraph of Story 3; students echo it back in unison. Repeat until end of story. (See **Echo Reading** in **Glossary**.)

ii. If good decoding and fluency are demonstrated, move on to feedback; if not, ask students to read a paragraph each.

Vocabulary – Oral

Rust the Robin can see the sill. **Sill** – is it:

a. windmill
b. window glass
[c. ledge below the window]

I ask you to tweet and trill. **Trill** – is it:

a. drill
[b. chirp]
c. shout

Dictation

Rust sees him and spits.

Tom Brown is just not thinking.

What fun to see you, up in that tall tree!

Rust sings proud and loud.

Comprehension – Oral Questions

Which words describe Rex the Fox: *sincere, dangerous, cunning, warm-hearted*?
[Dangerous, cunning.]

Is there any difference between Rust stealing the ham and Rex stealing the ham?
[Yes – in method (an opportunistic grab v calculated deception) and emotions (Rust's conscience tells her it's wrong).]

This is an Aesop's Fable, therefore it has a moral. What is the moral?
[Don't listen to flatterers.]

I Am Cat: Playing in the Tree

Reading

i. Ⓣ reads Poem 2 with prosody while students concentrate on visualizing the narrative rather than following the sounds with a pointer.
ii. Students then quietly read the poem in unison with T, placing pointer or finger under each word.
iii. If good decoding and fluency are demonstrated, move on to feedback; if not, cold call students to read a verse each.

Odd One Out

T dictates the following words; students write them down and circle the odd one out:

Grass, pond, rock, ground, greed, log, rat, cat, dog, stick, tree [greed]

Phoneme Substitution

play	*/l/ to /r/*	*[pray]*
stick	*/i/ to /a/*	*[stack]*
last	*/l/ to /f/*	*[fast]*
green	*/g/ to /p/*	*[preen]*
grim	*/m/ to /t/*	*[grit]*
run	*/n/ to /t/*	*[rut]*
pound	*/ou/ to /o/*	*[pond]*
bound	*/ou/ to /i/*	*[bind]*

Keep the Cat

Introducing

'ey' /ae/

Unusual spellings

s ai d s o me

Reading

i. **T** reads circa two minutes of Story 4.
ii. Students then quietly read the story in unison with T, placing pointer or finger under each word.
iii. If all students appear to have a good grasp of decoding and fluency, move on to feedback; if not, have students read a paragraph each until story is completed.

Comprehension – Oral Questions

What happens down the pit?
[p39 Men dig out the coal.]

Name the members of the West family.
[p41-42 Kit, Lil, Dick, Poll, Pip, Peg, Tess (take one name from as many students as possible).]

Dick is: bitter, cheery, angry, tactful, gentle, harassed, overworked?
[Bitter, angry, harassed, overworked.]

Week 1 Lesson 5: Consolidation

Recall Quiz

T: make it clear that this is a way to strengthen memory so students should not consult their books.

Can anyone remember the verse they memorized in Lesson One?
[p11-12.]

What is the most significant thing the cat did in its first poem?
[p12 Kill a rat.]

What is the most significant thing the cat did in its second poem?
[p36 Get stuck up a tree.]

The gods send the frogs two kings. What are they?
[p16 King Log and p18 King Stork.]

Name three species of animal in She Who Has Lots of Pals…
[p23-25 Rabbit, dog, horse, bull, sheep.]

Who steals Tom Brown's ham?
[p29 First Rust the Robin p30-31 then Rex the Fox.]

What is the West family argument about?
[p41-42 Whether or not to keep the cat after it stole Dick's fish.]

Tenses

T: "As you will remember from 'ing', a suffix is a letter or group of letters which is added to the end of a word to change its meaning or grammatical function. In *Keep the Cat*, the suffix 'ed' is introduced. This alters the tense of a word. *Jump* is the present tense (present simple). *Jumping* is also the present tense but it is present continuous. And *jumped* is the past tense (past simple). *I was jumping* is the past continuous." Ask pupils to use their show-me whiteboards to answer the following questions.

"I played tennis" – is this:
a. Present simple
[b. Past simple]
c. Past continuous

"I play tennis" – is this:
a. Present continuous
b. Past simple
[c. Present simple]

"I am playing tennis" – is this:
a. Past continuous
b. Present simple
[c. Present continuous]

"I was playing tennis" – is this:
a. Present continuous
[b. Past continuous]
c. Past simple

T to give several more examples if students are struggling.

"Note that there are three ways of pronouncing the suffix 'ed': /d/, /t/ and /id/. For example, 'ed' on the end of 'open' is 'open/d/'. 'Ed' on the end of 'help' is 'help/t/'. And 'ed' on the end of 'add' is 'add/id/.'"

Graphic Sequencing

Ask the students to draw lines over a double-page spread in their exercise books to divide it thus:

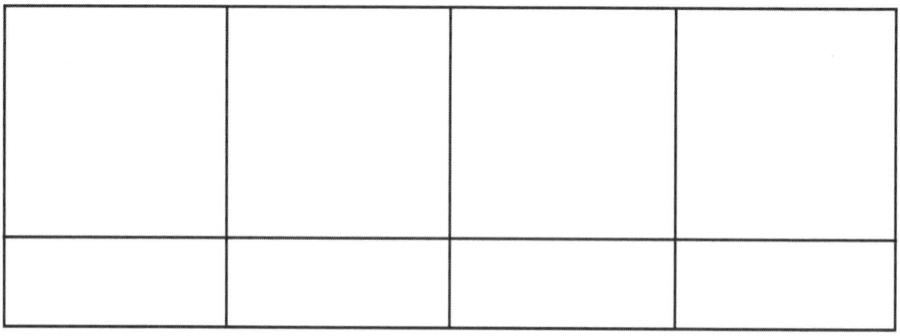

Or thus, depending on the type of exercise book:

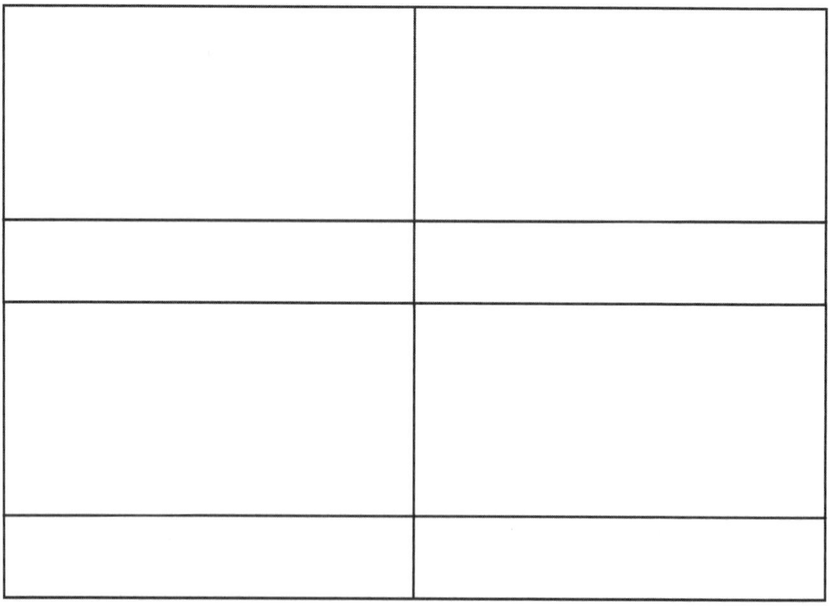

Ask students to pick four scenes from *The Frogs Demand a King* to write or copy a brief sentence about in the lower boxes and illustrate in black and white in the boxes above. Take time and care with this exercise. No need to rush. Sequencing is key.

Crossword

T puts crossword on whiteboard/visualizer for whole class, or photocopies crossword for individual use. Books to be kept shut at first as this is a recall challenge, though struggling students could be allowed a few minutes at the end to look for the answers.

*[**Across:** 2. Buttercup, 4. DickWest, 6. gods*
***Down:** 1. Rabbit, 3. Cat, 5. king, 7. Stork]*

Across

2. The sweetest cow in all the land

4. Man with ten kids

6. What frogs pray to

Down

1. Animal who brags about having lots of pals

3. Killer of rats

5. What frogs pray for

7. Killer of frogs

Week 2 Lesson 1: Sad Slim and Spitting Freda & King Midas

Sad Slim and Spitting Freda

Reading

i. Ⓣ reads Story 5 with prosody.
ii. Students then quietly read the story in unison with T, placing pointer or finger under each word.
iii. If good decoding and fluency are demonstrated by everyone, move on to feedback; if not, have students read a paragraph each until the story is completed.

Vocabulary – Oral

Slim the Slug basked in the sun. **Bask** – is it:

a. bathe
[b. sunbathe]
c. wriggle

No win for that preening frog! **Preen** – is it:

[a. primp]
b. green
c. wicked

Sagging and slumping. **Sag** – is it:

a. bag
b. sling
[c. droop]

Slump – is it:

[a. flop]
b. slip
c. dive

Comprehension – Oral Questions

What does Slim say about himself?
[p45 "I am a fun, fab, fit slug!"]

Do you think Slim really believes that he is a fun, fab, fit slug?
[p46 Probably not as he starts sobbing at the prospect of getting up a hill.]

What is Freda's attitude towards the ants?
[p46 Racist; Freda sneers at the thought of being friends with ants.]

What goes wrong for Freda?
[p46-47 She is tempted by a cool swim and a nice nap, prioritising them over the race due to over-confidence.]

This is an Aesop's Fable and therefore is all about the moral – what do you think the moral is?
[Slow and steady wins the race – i.e. it's better to be methodical than quick and careless.]

King Midas

Reading

i. Ⓣ reads Story 6 with prosody.
ii. Students then quietly read the story in unison with T, placing pointer or finger under each word.
iii. If good decoding and fluency are demonstrated by everyone, move on to feedback; if not, have students read a paragraph each until the story is completed.

Vocabulary – Oral

Shimmering gold. **Shimmer** – is it:

a. shower
[b. shine]
c. sombre

Feeling famished. **Famished** – is it:

a. famous
b. family-minded
[c. starving]

Dunked her in the pond. **Dunk** – is it:

a. swan
[b. duck]
c. goose

All that was not gold was dross. **Dross** – is it:

[a. dregs]
b. flashy
c. unreal

Sentence Reworking

T: write the following sentence on the whiteboard, reading it aloud: “You are the king of a big, well-off land. You are fit and strong. You are not thick.” Repeat the first segment (“You are the king of a big, well-off land”) and ask if anyone can rephrase this. Do the same for the two subsequent segments, modelling if necessary.
[You rule a large rich kingdom. You are healthy and powerful. You are also intelligent.]

Repeat for:

“And Midas stamped and stormed and kicked at the servant for being so frank.”
[And the King threw a temper tantrum at his attendant for being honest with him.]

“And the King was thrilled to bits… until, feeling famished, he grabbed a ham to sink his teeth into.”
[King Midas was utterly delighted … until, ravenous, he seized some pork to devour.]

Phoneme Substitution

sweet	*/ee/ to /o/*	*[swot]*
long	*/ng/ to /t/*	*[lot]*
heels	*/h/ to /f/*	*[feels]*
dunk	*/d/ to /h/*	*[hunk]*
crown	*/n/ to /d/*	*[crowd]*
yelp	*/p/ to /l/*	*[yell]*
king	*/ng/ to /ll/*	*[kill]*

Prosody: Word Emphasis

T models repeat reading of the sentence below, strongly emphasizing different word(s) each time. Thoroughly discuss how the emphasis changes the meaning, impact and/or implication of the sentence:

All King Midas longed for was gold.

All **King Midas** longed for was gold.

All King Midas **longed** for was gold.

All King Midas longed for was **gold**.

Comprehension – Oral Questions

How would you describe King Midas?
[Obsessive, greedy, excitable, powerful, impulsive.]

Describe the different emotions King Midas goes through.
[Yearning for gold; fury at the lack of gold; glee at the abundance of gold; shock at the pain of losing teeth; horror at the transformation of his daughter; relief and a bit of embarrassment at her restoration.]

What do you think the god's motivation is?
[As with The Frogs Demand a King *– to teach Midas to be careful what he wishes for.]*

Week 2 Lesson 2: Scorpion and Frog & Smug Rane and Zog the Frog

Scorpion and Frog

Reading

i. Ⓣ reads Story 7 with prosody.
ii. Students then quietly read the story in unison with T, placing pointer or finger under each word.
iii. If good decoding and fluency are demonstrated, move on to feedback; if not, ask students to read a paragraph each.

Vocabulary – Oral

Sog pondered this. **Ponder** – is it:
a. gobble
b. love
[c. consider]

You'll perish as well. **Perish** – is it:
a. shrivel
[b. die]
c. danger

Okay, so we may *be a tad malignant.* **Malignant** – is it:
a. handsome
b. unhappy
[c. evil]

Vocabulary – Written

T writes the list below on the board: students read each word in unison with T before copying down the two columns and circling the odd word out in each column.

malignant	*luck*
sting	*toxic*
horrid	*kind*
talent	*protect*
monster	*confident*
sadistic	*content*

[talent and toxic as they are nice and nasty words respectively.]

Prosody: Word Emphasis

(See p41 for instructions.)

“**You** don’t understand,” shrugged the scorpion as he drowned.

“You **don’t** understand,” shrugged the scorpion as he drowned.

“You don’t **understand**,” shrugged the scorpion as he drowned.

“You don’t understand,” shrugged **the scorpion** as he drowned.

“You don’t understand,” shrugged the scorpion as he **drowned**.

Phoneme Substitution

drown	*/d/ to /c/*	*[crown]*
think	*/th/ to /l/*	*[link]*

nutter	*/n/ to /b/*	*[butter]*
seem	*/m/ to /d/*	*[seed]*
seem	*/ee/ to /u/*	*[sum]*
snug	*/n/ to /m/*	*[smug]*
then	*/th/ to /h/*	*[hen]*

Comprehension – Oral Questions

What does Zing the Scorpion ask of Sog the Frog?
[p57 to give him a lift across a pond.]

What is Sog's first reaction to Zing's request? How does it change, and why?
[p57-58 Sog utterly refuses out of fear for his life. When Zing argues that hurting Sog would cost him his own life, Sog first considers this and then agrees.]

Why does Zing kill himself and Sog?
[p59 It is his nature to kill whatever the cost; he just can't help himself.]

Smug Rane and Zog the Frog

Introducing

'a-e' /ae/
'i-e' /ie/

T: "So far we have encountered one or two letters making a single sound. For example, 'a' is /a/ and 's' 'h' is /sh/. Now we have two letters that have been split up but still only make one sound. For example: 'Hat' is pronounced /h/ /a/ /t/ – 'hat'. If we add an 'e' on the end, it joins up with its fellow vowel 'a' so the word becomes /h/ /ae/ /t/ – 'hate'." T writes other examples on whiteboard whilst saying the words with exaggerated /ae/ sounds: *ape, cake, game, brave, plane.*

"As well as introducing a separate 'a' and 'e' as an /ae/ sound, this story introduces a separate 'i' and 'e' as an /ie/ sound. For example:" – T writes on whiteboard whilst saying the words with exaggerated /ie/ sounds: *kite, pine, prize, wife, dive.*

"Finally, this story introduces another function of the apostrophe. Previously we used it to shorten words – for instance, *'She is' becoming 'She's'* [write 'She is → She's' on whiteboard whilst saying this]. However, the apostrophe also functions as a *possessive.* 'The husband of Ann' becomes 'Ann's husband' [write 'The husband of Ann → Ann's husband' on whiteboard whilst saying this. Do the same for 'the lake of King Jake' becoming 'King Jake's lake']."

Background Knowledge

The Princess and the Frog was the favourite tale of German legend-collectors the Brothers Grimm. The Prince and Princess are pressurised into a relationship, regardless of his lack of any defining characteristic other than "No-longer-Frog" and her dishonesty, immaturity and selfishness.

Reading

i. T reads first paragraph; students echo it back in unison. Repeat until end of story.
ii. If good decoding and fluency are demonstrated, move on to feedback; if not, have students read a paragraph each.

Writing/Copying

T writes the following three lines on the whiteboard for students to copy, concentrating on their handwriting:

Zog rises from the rocks and the weeds of the lake.

"Shame on you!" says her dad the King, frowning.

Five times Zog dives into the lake.

Ask students to reread the first paragraph of p63 and write down every example of an 'a-e' and 'i-e' word they can find, drawing a connecting arc above the two vowels – e.g. Jake.

[side, Jake, late, life, wife, Rane, lime, time, lake]

Grammar

If students have completed the MRI Level 1 Lesson Plans, refresh their memories of its Basic Grammar lessons. If they haven't, introduce the concepts of nouns, verbs, adverbs and adjectives. (See **Appendix C.**)

T writes the words below on the whiteboard and asks students to write them down in two columns, one entitled *Noun* and one entitled *Verb.*

swims Zog plays slips drop sob rises begs dives sing king lake thinks jump Rane hop pouts kiss lane sniffs Jake mime fortress smiles

*[**Noun:** Zog, king, lake, Rane, lane, Jake, fortress **Verb:** swims, plays, slips, drop, sob, rises, begs, dives, sing, thinks, jump, hop, pouts, kiss, sniffs, mime, smiles.]*

Fill the Blanks

T writes the words *talent, snack, **lime, lake,** sh**ame*** on the board and slowly reads them aloud, asking students to echo each word in unison before conducting a brief discussion of them. Erase the words, replacing them with the sentences below. Ask students to copy out at least three of these lines and fill in the blanks with the words just discussed, without consulting the text. (Note double length of the underscore for sounds with two letters.) T circulates, checking student work and if necessary modelling the correct answer(s).

Five times Zog dives into the _ _ _ _. *[lake]*

We scorpions do relish a tempting _ _ _ __. *[snack]*

Zog is a _ _ _ _-green frog. *[lime]*

Swimming is not my biggest _ _ _ _ _ _! *[talent]*

"__ _ _ _ on you!" says her dad the King, frowning. *[Shame]*

Week 2 Lesson 3: Hal Rex

Background Knowledge

"Divorced, beheaded, died; divorced, beheaded, survived" is how Henry VIII's six wives are remembered. Henry's tyrannical nature, inconsistency in love, war and religion, and obsession with begetting a son to secure the Tudor dynasty resulted in a tumultuous reign.

The Lump

Reading

i. Ⓣ reads Story 9 Part 1 with prosody.
ii. Students quietly read the story in unison with T, placing pointer or finger under each word.
iii. Each student reads a paragraph until story is completed.
iv. T provides feedback as necessary.

Phoneme Substitution

sink	*/n/ to /l/*	*[silk]*
still	*/ll/ to /ff/*	*[stiff]*
kick	*/ck/ to /ss/*	*[kiss]*
strong	*/o/ to /i/*	*[string]*
lump	*/l/ to /b/*	*[bump]*
shame	*/m/ to /d/*	*[shade]*

The Wives

Reading

i. Ⓣ reads Story 9 Part 2 with prosody.
ii. Students quietly read the story in unison with T, placing pointer or finger under each word.
iii. Each student reads a paragraph until story is completed.
iv. T provides feedback as necessary.

Vocabulary – Oral

This was a bit arrogant. **Arrogant** – is it:
[a. self-important]
b. modest
c. stupid

It was a dank prison. **Dank** – is it:
a. large
[b. damp]
c. spooky

Hal said she was a strumpet. **Strumpet** – is it:
a. harpy
[b. prostitute]
c. madwoman

Vocabulary – Homonyms

Ⓣ: "'Rank' is one of those words with several completely different meanings (a *homonym*). Can anyone give me a definition for the word 'rank'? Can anyone give me another definition?"
[Stinking (the meat had gone off and was rank); position in society

(he held the rank of Duke); position in the army (he was promoted to the rank of Brigadier); complete (a rank amateur); row (they stood in ranks of ten).]

The King

Reading

i. Ⓣ reads Story 9 Part 3 with prosody.
ii. Students quietly read the story in unison with T, placing pointer or finger under each word.
iii. Each student reads a paragraph until story is completed.
iv. T provides feedback as necessary.

Vocabulary – Oral

The gash in his leg that cannot be mended. **Gash** – is it:

a. smash
b. stitches
[c. wound]

And hacked to bits. **Hack** – is it:

a. pull
b. push
[c. chop]

Hal yells with the gout. **Gout** – is it:

a. headache
[b. painful joint disease]
c. painful eye disease

How they had vexed him. **Vex** – is it:

[a. annoy]
b. comfort
c. delight

How fleet her feet! **Fleet** – is it:

a. flat
b. plump
[c. speedy]

Fill the Blanks

T writes *red, gold, black, slim, fleet* on board and slowly reads them aloud, asking students to echo each word in unison. T wipes the board and writes the following sentences (minus the answers in square brackets):

How _____ her lips! *[red]*

How _____ her legs! *[slim]*

How _____ her feet! *[fleet]*

How _____ her locks! *[red* **or** *gold* **or** *black]*

T asks students to copy out the sentences, filling in the blanks with the appropriate word.

Comprehension – Oral Questions

Why are the king's courtiers lying?
[p69-71 From fear – both of Henry and of the uncertain post-Henry future with a child monarch.]

What is the reaction to the "joke" about the King taking another wife, and why?

[p70-71 Horror, due to the disasters of the previous marriages that frequently ended with headless queens and courtiers.]

What a sad jest it was when Ann had a lass – why?
[p73 King Henry thought only a male could rule. (He had spent six years trying to divorce Queen Katherine, risking a civil war in the hope of breeding a son with his beloved Anne Boleyn.)]

Week 2 Lesson 4: Hanging Nate Part 1

Introducing

'o-e' /oe/ 'ore' /or/

T: "As you will remember, a separate 'a' and 'e' can make a single /ae/ sound, as in 'Kate'. And a separate 'i' and 'e' can make a single /ie/ sound, as in 'dive'. This story now introduces a separate 'o' and 'e' as an /oe/ sound. For example, *nose, smoke, doze*. [Write these on whiteboard, with an arc linking the 'o-e's.] It also introduces the letters 'o' 'r' 'e', sound /or/. For example, *bore, shore, core, gore, wore.* [Write these on whiteboard, underlining 'ore'.]"

Reading

i. Ⓣ reads the first part of *Nate the Brave* with prosody (to penultimate paragraph of p82).
ii. Students quietly read the first half of *Nate the Brave* (to p84 paragraph 3) in unison with T.
iii. Students quietly read the second half of *Nate the Brave* in unison with T.
iv. T provides feedback as necessary.

Characterization

Ⓣ writes *Nate the <u>Brave</u>, Jack <u>Bald-Pate</u>, <u>Lame</u> Nick, Beth the <u>Bold</u>, <u>Pocked</u> Sam, Dan the <u>Lump</u>, Nip the <u>Dog</u>, Smoke the <u>Steed</u>* on the board. "Name one other fact about any of these characters." Instruct students to reread the passage in unison if they don't recall enough facts.
[p82 paras 2-7.]

Vocabulary – Oral

So I'm a sham, am I? **Sham** – is it:
a. shanty
b. shame
[c. fraud]

Hold, you rascal! **Rascal** – is it:
[a. scoundrel]
b. thief
c. murderer

Who made you a despot? **Despot** – is it:
a. desperate person
[b. dictator]
c. gambler

A bit of a lout. **Lout** – is it:

a. a loud person

b. a quiet person

[c. a brutish person]

Bling from fops. **Fop** – is it:

a. a floppy person

[b. a vain, foolish person]

c. a foreign person

The bleeding was stemmed. **Stemmed** – is it:

[a. stopped]

b. scarlet

c. encouraged

Phoneme Substitution

lout	*/t/ to /d/*	*[loud]*
fang	*/f/ to /b/*	*[bang]*
black	*/b/ to /c/*	*[clack]*
swore	*/w/ to /n/*	*[snore]*
growl	*/g/ to /p/*	*[prowl]*
lame	*/l/ to /d/*	*[dame]*
drunk	*/u/ to /a/*	*[drank]*

Scrambled Sentences

T writes the words below on the board and asks students to rearrange them to make sentences:

jacket he his rags hacked into

gang crowd sang the his of

gang endless the was job an feeding

out luck Brave's Nate the ran

songs deeds made his of minstrels

Week 2 Lesson 5: Consolidation

Recall Quiz

T: Make it clear that this is a way to strengthen memory so students should not consult their books.

Name the two creatures who take part in a race.
[p45 Slim the Slug and Freda the Frog.]

What is King Midas's favourite thing in the world?
[p53 It actually turns out to be his daughter rather than gold.]

How does Scorpion persuade Frog to take him across the pond?
[p58 By pointing out that killing him would kill them both.]

How does Rane break her word?
[p64-65 She didn't take the Frog as her pet as she had promised.]

What has King Hal got against his wives?
[p77 Too few sons and too much nagging. Plus suspected infidelity and witchcraft.]

Name the members of Nate's gang.
[p82 Nate the Brave, Jack Bald-Pate, Lame Nick, Beth the Bold, Pocked Sam, Dan the Lump, Nip the Dog, Smoke the Steed. Take one name from as many students as possible.]

Phoneme Breakdown

(See p16 for instructions.)

Remind students that the suffix 'ed' can be pronounced in three different ways, i.e. 'open' → 'open/d/', 'help' → 'help/t/' and 'add' → 'add/id/.' /id/ counts as two different sounds.

mend	*[4*	*m e n d]*
never	*[4*	*n e v **er**]*
limp	*[4*	*l i m p]*
stomp	*[5*	*s t o m p]*
fresh	*[4*	*f r e **sh**]*
clown	*[4*	*c l **ow** n]*
fibbed	*[4*	*f i **bb** **ed**]*
running	*[5*	*r u **nn** i **ng**]*
spotted	*[6*	*s p o **tt** e d]*
hanging	*[5*	*h a **ng** i **ng**]*

Fill the Blanks

T writes the words *sweet, scorpions, ground, crown, fangs, playing* on the board, and slowly reads them aloud, asking students to echo each word in unison before conducting a brief discussion of them. Erase the words, replacing them with the sentences below. Ask students to copy out at least three of these lines and fill in the blanks with the appropriate words, without consulting the text.

Rane is sitting in the sun _ _ __ _ __ games. *[playing]*

We _ _ __ _ _ _ _ _ _ prefer dry desert sands to horrid ponds. *[scorpions]*

Bess was as fit for the _ _ __ _ as Hal was not. *[crown]*

What luck that we met, my _ _ __ _ duck! *[sweet]*

Nip the Dog with her long _ _ __ _. *[fangs]*

He fell to the _ _ __ _ _. *[ground]*

Vocabulary – Positive or Negative

T: ask students to divide a page into two columns, headed with a "+" to represent the positive words and a "-" to represent the negative ones. Dictate each word in the list below, repeating each one with an emphasis on every syllable. Ask students to write them down in the correct column. Discuss any common errors with the whole class afterwards. Ask which character they think the negative traits are based on. *[Zing the Scorpion.]*

*[**Positive:** helpful, kind, sweet. **Negative:** toxic, malignant, stinging, sadistic, brutal.]*

Syllable Chunking

(See p26 for instructions.)

ex pose, out land ish, sculpt ing, Scot land, be fall en, arr o gant, vex ed, mal ig nant, scorp i on, sad is tic

Crossword

Ⓣ puts crossword on whiteboard/visualizer for whole class, or photocopies crossword for individual use. Books to be kept shut at first as this is a recall challenge, though struggling students could be allowed a few minutes at the end to look for the answers.

*[**Across:** 3. bandit, 5. Jane, 7. wives*
***Down:** 1. Midas, 2. Rane, 4. Kate, 6. Zing]*

Across

3. Nate's job

5. Mother of Hal Rex's lad

7. What Hal Rex had six of

Down

1. King obsessed with gold

2. Princess with a Frog

4. Hal Rex's last bride

6. Scorpion

Week 3 Lesson 1: Hanging Nate Part 2 & Space Race

Nate the Not-So-Brave

Reading

i. T reads the first half of Story 10 Part 2 (to bottom of p88) with prosody, students following, placing pointer or finger under each word.
ii. Students quietly read first half of story in unison with T, placing pointer or finger under each word.
iii. T reads first sentence of p89, and students immediately echo in unison. Repeat for remainder of story.
iv. T provides feedback as necessary.

Vocabulary – Oral

Nate the Not-So-Brave who had wavered. **Waver** – is it:

a. wave
b. weave
[c. hesitate]

This lad led astray. **Astray** – is it:

a. a stray pet
b. in the right moral direction
[c. in the wrong moral direction]

Old pals slunk away. **Slunk** – is it:

a. a skunk
[b. a furtive movement]
c. storming out

I'm a sham, am I. **Sham** – is it:

[a. a fraud]
b. ashamed
c. a hero

Memorization

T: Allow students ten minutes to memorise the first three verses on p87 before pairing them up to recite to each other.

Comprehension – Oral Questions

Students to use show-me whiteboard for answers.

A big lump of Jack's leg came off – is this description:

a. bland
[b. dramatic]
c. realistic

"Oh, bad luck," said Beth, attempting to seem sad – is Beth:

a. guilt-ridden
b. genuinely sympathetic
[c. sarcastic]

Nor did Nate wish to go down in combat, all guns blazing – is Nate:

[a. depressed]
b. angry
c. serene

Nate went to his hanging with a wave and a joke – is Nate:

a. respectful
b. petrified
[c. defiant]

Comprehension – Oral Discussion

Discuss the characteristics of Nate.
[Reckless, greedy, charismatic, brave, popular, ruthless, rogue, criminal, exploitative, gallant, apathetic.]

Space Race

Introducing

'ze', /z/ 'ce', /s/

Reading

i. Ⓣ reads Poem 3, emphasising the drama and rhythm.
ii. Students quietly read the story in unison with T, placing pointer or finger under each word.
iii. T provides feedback as necessary.

Vocabulary – Oral

It lopes on ten legs. **Lopes** – is it:
a. flees
[b. canters]
c. limps

And the orbiting globes. **Orbit** – is it:
[a. rotate]
b. fly
c. swim

Globe – is it:

a. square

b. rectangle

[c. sphere]

Week 3 Lesson 2: The Ice Lass

The Ice Lass: Madness

Introducing

'u-e' /oo/

Unusual spellings

l o ve p ure

Reading

i. Ⓣ reads Story 11 Part 1 with prosody.

ii. Students quietly read the story in unison with T, placing pointer or finger under each word.

iii. Students read a few sentences each until Part 1 is completed.

iv. T provides feedback as necessary.

Vocabulary – Oral

Sculpting her small feet. **Sculpt** – is it:
a. scalp
b. scale
[c. carve]

This outlandish thing. **Outlandish** – is it:
a. the outback
b. landlocked
[c. bizarre]

The kids outside make an ice hag. **Hag** – is it:
a. a large bag
[b. an ugly old woman]
c. an ugly old man

Comprehension – Oral Questions

What form does Oleg and Olga's madness take?
[p100 Building a girl of snow and hoping she comes alive.]

How do Oleg and Olga first react to the Ice Lass?
[p101 Clapping, sobbing, thanking the gods, hugging and patting her, dressing her, taking her indoors.]

The Ice Lass: Loss

Reading

i. Students quietly read Story 11 Part 2 in unison with Ⓣ, placing pointer or finger under each word.

ii. If reading is fluent, provide feedback and move on; if not, every student reads a paragraph until passage is complete.

Characterization

Ⓣ writes the following characteristics on the whiteboard and asks students to copy them into two columns, one headed "Ice Lass" and the other headed "NOT Ice Lass": *shy, stubborn, clever, fast, timid, brave, outlandish, obedient, strong-minded.*

*[**Ice Lass:** stubborn, clever, fast, brave, outlandish, strong-minded.*
***Not Ice Lass:** shy, timid, obedient.]*

Comprehension – Oral Questions

Name the creatures that the Ice Lass encountered while stuck in the tree.
[p103-104 Sleek panther, huge snake, red fox.]

How and why do Olga and Oleg lose their daughter?
[p106 She melts because the magic is broken as soon as she thinks her parents love her less.]

You love me less than you love that hen – do you think this is a fair judgement?
[p106 No, Olga and Oleg just thought they could have both.]

Vocabulary

What tore at Olga and Oleg… dragging them down, bleeding them of gladness – which of these words convey the tragedy of the couple's childlessness?
[Tore, dragging, bleeding.]

T: "*The Ice Lass scaled a tall ash tree* – 'scale' is a homonym. Who remembers what the word 'homonym' means? Can anyone think of any of the various different meanings for 'scale'?"
[Climb (scale a tree), relative size (e.g. of a map), a weighing instrument (bathroom scales), a piece of the skin of some scaly creatures (fish scales), deposit left by boiling water (descale your kettle!), a sequence of musical notes (practice your scales!).]

Week 3 Lesson 3: Macbeth

Background Knowledge

Regarded as the world's greatest writer, William Shakespeare (1564-1616) was an actor from Stratford-upon-Avon. He wrote 38 plays – histories, tragedies and comedies. He also wrote two narrative poems and 154 sonnets, to a Fair Youth as well as a Dark Lady.

Shakespeare's play *Macbeth* is a highly-fictionalised account of real events in eleventh-century Scotland. We know little of the reign of the real King Macbeth – Mac Bethad mac Findlaích, the "Red King" – but the few contemporary records that survive speak favourably of him as "generous" and "renowned". He reigned for seventeen years, went on a pilgrimage to Rome during which he gave extravagantly to the poor, and adopted his stepson as his heir, before his line was defeated by Malcolm III.

Actors have a superstitious belief that uttering the play's name will lead to disaster, so refer to it as "The Scottish Play".

Introducing

/er/ 'ur'
/ar/ 'ar'
/g/ 'gh'
/air/ 'ere'

NB: The names of some of the characters have been adapted to match the current level of Alphabetic Code knowledge.

Synopsis

T: "Reading is a combination of decoding and comprehension. As I would like you to concentrate on giving a really good dramatic reading of the text, I'm now going to summarise the first half of the play so that it'll be easier to follow what's going on and who's who.

"The play opens after a battle – there has been a rebellion against old King Duncan of Scotland and loyal Lord Macbeth has led the King's army to victory, personally killing the rebel leader in a sword-fight. Returning home with his good friend Lord Ban (Banquo), they meet three witches who claim to be able to see the future – that Macbeth will become King of Scotland and that Ban's descendants will also be Kings. Macbeth doesn't know what to believe – or to do about it – but when he confides in his wife, she is quite sure that they should kill King Duncan to ensure that this 'happy' event comes about. She bullies Macbeth into this horrendous crime and it works – Duncan's son Mal runs away for fear of also being killed and Macbeth is chosen as Scotland's new King.

"Having committed one murder, Macbeth finds it quite easy to order more, propelled by his jealousy and fear that *Ban* would father the future royal Scottish line. Things start to go wrong when Ban's son escapes his assassin – and Ban's ghost turns up at Macbeth's coronation banquet. As it's a figment of Macbeth's guilty imagination, only he is able to see it. Despite his wife's attempts to brush his screaming horror under the carpet, the most important lords of the realm have seen that their King's sanity is in doubt."

Reading

i. T selects eleven students – one for each character (Ban, Macbeth, Hag 1, Hag 2, Hag 3, Dame Macbeth, King Duncan, Prince Mal, King's Man, Killer) plus the narrator. If not enough students, give more than one minor part to one person; if too many students, assign different actors for the second half of the play.

ii. Allow students time to look through the first half of the play (to end p117) and highlight their own parts if necessary. Everyone except the Macbeths and Ban should read the "ALL" lines on p116-117.

iii. Students dramatically read their own lines (to end p117), whilst being careful to follow all readings with finger or pointer as usual.

iv. T provides feedback as necessary and models passages that have lacked dramatic effect in the students' reading.

Comprehension – Oral Questions

Why is Macbeth hailed as a hero at first?
[p109 He's just won a battle, saving King Duncan by defeating a rebel army.]

What is Macbeth's initial reactions on being told to murder the King?
[p111-112 Incredulity; horror; stammering hesitation.]

Why does Macbeth order the murder of Ban and his son?
[p115 To avert the hags' prophecy that Ban's descendants, not Macbeth's, would become the royal line of Scotland.]

Characterization

T writes *sweet, ruthless, placid, spineless, spiteful, hesitant, power-crazed, pitiless, brutal, brave, wimp, helpful, bland* on the board whilst saying the words. T then asks students to divide a page into two columns – *Macbeth* and *Dame Macbeth* – before asking students to write down each word in the correct column. Make it clear that some words will apply to both characters and some to neither. Circle the room providing feedback during the task. Thoroughly discuss students' differing interpretations afterwards, with emphasis on the complexity of Macbeth's character and the fact it shifts over time, meaning that he can be both brave and spineless, helpful and ruthless.

*[**Macbeth:** brave, helpful, spineless, hesitant (early on) and ruthless, power-crazed, pitiless (later on). **Dame Macbeth:** ruthless, spiteful, power-crazed, pitiless, brutal, brave (?). **Neither option:** sweet, placid, bland.]*

Phoneme Reversal

T: "Instead of changing one of the sounds in a word, we will now be reversing all the sounds in a word." Say each of the words in the left-hand column below aloud and cold call a student to reverse it. Model the first word.

gab	*[bag]*
dog	*[god]*
snug	*[guns]*
pals	*[slap]*
pat	*[tap]*
mug	*[gum]*
nuts	*[stun]*

Week 3 Lesson 4: Macbeth (cont.)

Synopsis

🅣 "Macbeth is freaked-out not just by the appearance of a ghost but by the fact that the powerful Lord Macduff of Fife has boycotted his coronation. He decides to consult the witches again. They confirm that Macduff will betray him, but they also state that no man born of woman can ever harm Macbeth, and that he shall not be defeated until the woods start walking. Macbeth is greatly reassured… until the witches' refusal to withdraw their previous prophecy concerning the descendants of Ban being Kings.

"Macbeth resolves to kill Macduff just to be on the safe side, and on learning that he's already fled, sends an assassin to slaughter Macduff's family instead. Macduff – now in England attempting to inspire Prince Mal to raise an army and retake Scotland from the tyrant – is naturally devastated when the news of the assassination reaches him.

"Lady Macbeth is being driven insane by her guilt, unable to scrub her hands clean of imaginary blood. With the army of Mal and Macduff approaching, her husband has little time to console her – or even to react with anything more than brief despair when she commits suicide.

"As he leads his army into battle, Macbeth is still confident, thanks to the witches' promises, that he can never be defeated. Until he realises that the prophecy about walking woods has been fulfilled by the approaching army camouflaging itself with leaves and branches. But at least he can never be killed... until Macduff, engaging him in a sword-fight, reveals that he was delivered via caesarean section from his dead mother's body rather than, technically speaking, being *born* of woman. Realising he is doomed, Macbeth cries 'Lay on, Macduff, And damn'd be him that first cries, "Hold, enough!"' He is duly slain and Mal hailed as King in his place."

Reading

i. Choose three students to play Dame Macduff, Macduff and Ross. Allow students time to look through the second half of the play (p118 onwards), highlighting their own parts, if necessary.
ii. Students dramatically read their own lines (p118 onwards), whilst being careful to follow all readings with finger or pointer as usual.
iii. T provides feedback as necessary and models passages that have lacked dramatic effect in the students' reading.

Vocabulary – Oral Questions

Fakes. They must *have been fakes* – what is another word for "fakes"?
[Frauds, conwomen, impostors, phonies.]

Sick with odd whims that will not let her sleep – what is another word for "whim"?
[Fancies, dreams, nightmares, fantasies.]

No mere cry can disturb me, not after the things I've seen! – what is another word for "disturb"?
[Frighten, upset, alarm, unnerve.]

Comprehension – Oral Questions

What does Macbeth mean when he calls Macduff "Judas"?
[It's a reference to the Biblical betrayal of Jesus Christ by his disciple Judas Iscariot, who sold him to the authorities for thirty pieces of silver. Judas later hanged himself in remorse.]

Why is Macbeth displeased by his second encounter with the hags?
[p118-119 They refuse to withdraw their claim that Ban, not himself, will father future Scottish royalty.]

Well, if I cannot murder Macduff, I think I'll murder his wife and kids. That seems wise – how has Macbeth changed since the beginning of the play?
[From horror and doubt at the prospect of murder to utter casualness. (As Lord Acton said, "Power tends to corrupt, and absolute power corrupts absolutely.")]

And now he betrays me? Just cos I killed the King – which of these emotions is Macbeth definitely NOT feeling: *aggrieved,*

puzzled, satisfied, hurt, angry?
[Satisfied.]

Embrace the fate of this dark time is a euphemism for what?
[Murder.]

Fill the Blanks

T writes the "words" below on the board and asks students to fill in the blanks with the appropriate letters – either 'a' 'r' for the /ar/ sound (as in hard) or 'u' 'r' for the /er/ sound (as in turn). They should write 'ar' or 'ur' on their whiteboards and hold them up as the teacher taps each word.

d__k	*[ar]*
abs__d	*[ur]*
st__t	*[ar]*
c__d*	*[ar], [ur]*
sh__k	*[ar]*
j__	*[ar]*
f__*	*[ar], [ur]*
l__k*	*[ar], [ur]*
c__l	*[ur]*

*Either is correct (*card/curd, far/fur, lark/lurk*).

Week 3 Lesson 5: Consolidation

Recall Quiz

T: make it clear that this is a way to strengthen memory so students should not consult their books.

Why does Nate's popularity change?
[p87, p91 Firstly it plummets because he left a lad to die and then it rises due to his deathbed courage.]

Where does the starship go?
[p95-96 Space; monster-ridden planets; icy and fiery planets.]

Why does the Ice Lass melt?
[p106 Because she thinks her parents love a hen more than her.]

Name the three kings in *Macbeth*.
[p109 Duncan, p115 Macbeth, p124 Mal.]

Which two things did the hags promise Macbeth that made him believe he was invincible?
[p118 That no man born of woman could defeat him, and that nothing could defeat him until trees start walking.]

Vocabulary – Positive or Negative

T writes *betray, crush, murder, wise, brave, terrorist, brutish, vile, love, pride, hero, wimp, glad, dire, nice, fine, anger, shame, sweet, gore, disturb, darkness, spite* on the board whilst saying the words. T then asks students to divide a page into two columns, headed "+" and "-" to represent

positive and negative words. Model the first word before asking students to carefully write down each word in the correct column, whispering each sound as they do so and paying attention to handwriting. Circle the room providing feedback during the task. Discuss any disagreements – for example, "pride" can be a very positive trait but is condemned as one of the Seven Deadly Sins in Christianity.
*[**Positive:** wise, brave, love, hero, glad, nice, fine, sweet, pride.
Negative: betray, crush, murder, terrorist, brutish, vile, wimp, dire, anger, shame, gore, disturb, darkness, spite.]*

Fill the Blanks

T writes the words *trusted, bursting, terrorists, dagger, murder* on the board and slowly reads them aloud, asking students to echo each word in unison before conducting a brief discussion of them. Erase the words, replacing them with the sentences below. Ask students to copy out at least three of these lines and fill in the blanks with the words just discussed, without consulting the text. (Note the double length of the underscore for sounds with two letters.) T circulates, checking student work and if necessary modelling the correct answer(s).

Is this a _ _ __ __ I see before me? *[dagger]*

If I cannot _ __ _ __ Macduff, I think I'll _ __ _ __ his wife and kids. *[murder]*

The King is _ __ _ _ _ __ with pride in me. *[bursting]*

But I'm a _ _ _ _ _ _ _ lord. *[trusted]*

We thrashed the _ _ __ __ _ _ _ _! *[terrorists]*

Phoneme Reversal

(See p69 for instructions.)

pots *[stop]*

peek *[keep]*

buns *[snub]*

gab *[bag]*

keep *[peek]*

pal *[lap]*

maps *[spam]*

pets *[step]*

Crossword

(See p35 for instructions.)

*[**Across:** 2. Duncan, 3. breeze, 6. IceLass, 7. dagger*
***Down:** 1. Nate, 2. darkness, 4. Pip, 5. Macduff]*

Across

2. King killed by Macbeth

3. Freeze in the _____!

6. Olga and Olegs's offspring

7. How Macbeth kills the King

Down

1. Hanged by the King's men

2. "All of life has led the way to dust and _____."

4. Shot by the King's men

5. "Lay on, _____!"

Week 4 Lesson 1: Macbeth (cont.)

Reading

i. T selects any *Macbeth* passages that students struggled with and reads them out a sentence at a time, with students repeating each line in unison.
ii. T provides feedback as necessary.

Sentence Reworking

Ⓣ: write the following sentence on the whiteboard, reading it aloud: "Before the bat has flapped its wings, there shall be done a deed of dire note." Repeat the first segment ("Before the bat has flapped its wings") and ask if anyone can rephrase this. Do the same for the second half of the sentence, modelling if necessary.

[Before nightfall (NB: bats are nocturnal creatures) something terrible and significant will have occurred.]

Repeat for:

"Oh brave Macbeth, who waved his steel and cut a path to the brutish terrorist, and cut him from top to bottom."
[Oh bold Macbeth who swung his sword, and hacked through the army to the rebel leader, and sliced him in half.]

"Stop shaking gore-splattered locks at me!"
[Cease waving your blood-covered hair at me!]

"Macbeth shall not be crushed till the trees start strolling around!"
[King Macbeth will not be defeated until a wood begins walking.]

Comprehension – Oral Discussion

If fate will have me as king, why then, fate may crown me – what does this mean?
[That Macbeth thinks he doesn't need to take action like murdering the king – his destiny will unfold naturally.]

The hags' promise to Macbeth is a *self-fulfilling prophecy*. What do you understand by this term?
[That a prediction came true only because belief in it changed the future, not because it was predestined.]

Don't fret, my pet, until you celebrate the deed. What does this line tell you about the shifting relationship between the Macbeths?
[As soon as he's crowned, Macbeth goes from subservience towards his wife to treating her with condescension and no longer confiding in her.]

Macbeth committed a triple crime when he killed Duncan: it was the cold-blooded murder of: a. an innocent, helpless, sleeping old man, b. the divinely-appointed King to whom he has sworn loyalty and c. a guest under his roof at a time when hospitality was sacred. Which do you think was worst?
[Probably b. as the peace and security of the realm depended on fulfilling your obligation to those "above" and "below" you.]

I didn't kill you, Ban!... Nothing to disturb you, my lords – the King has small outbursts now and then... Ah, what a shame my sweet pal Ban didn't make it – discuss the various types of lie.
[The first a blatant, outright lie (Macbeth didn't wield the knife but did order Ban's murder); "small outbursts" is a spin-doctor-like underplaying of insanity that amounts to a lie; and "What a shame" is gloating hypocrisy given that if Macbeth had actually

wanted Ban at the banquet he could have just... not murdered him.]

In Shakespeare's original play, the new King Malcolm (Mal) refers to the Macbeths as "This dead butcher and his fiend-like Queen." Do you agree?
[Of course Malcolm was right that the Macbeths were monsters, but they were not as devoid of scruples as "butcher" and "fiend" imply: he was driven to hallucinations and she to madness and death by their guilty consciences.]

Language

Students read penultimate paragraph of p123 in unison. T then reads Shakespeare's original version of the speech:

"Tomorrow, and tomorrow, and tomorrow,
Creeps in this petty pace from day to day,
To the last syllable of recorded time;
And all our yesterdays have lighted fools
The way to dusty death. Out, out, brief candle!
Life's but a walking shadow, a poor player,
That struts and frets his hour upon the stage,
And then is heard no more. It is a tale
Told by an idiot, full of sound and fury,
Signifying nothing."

Discuss how the power and the poetry of the words convey Macbeth's absolute despair.

Week 4 Lesson 2: Crying Wolf

Introducing

/er/ 'ir' /u/ 'o' /00/ 'o'

Reading

i. 🅣 reads Story 12 with prosody.
ii. Students quietly read the story in unison with T, placing pointer or finger under each word.
iii. T provides feedback as necessary.
iv. Students read a paragraph of the story each until it's complete.
v. T provides feedback as necessary.

Vocabulary – Oral

Keen to clobber the bad wolf. **Clobber** – is it:

a. meet
[b. beat]
c. greet

Birt's job was to tend the sheep. **Tend** – is it:

a. herd
b. eat
[c. look after]

Down in the vale. **Vale** – is it:

a. town

b. village

[c. valley]

Stale, humdrum weeks. **Humdrum** – is it:

[a. monotonous]

b. musical

c. magical

Comprehension – Oral Questions

Birt is feeling:

a. content

[b. fed up]

c. hungry

Jeff is feeling:

a. proud

b. serene

[c. upset]

Birt is:

a. a cowherd

b. a swineherd

[c. a shepherd]

Birt cries "WOLF!" because:

a. he's bored

b. he wants payback

c. there is a wolf

[d. all of the above]

Dictation

Birt's job was to tend the sheep on the hill.

They creep, and lurk, and nip, and bark.

Birt sat slumped on a rock as his dad started back down the hill.

Odd One Out

T dictates the following words for students to write down, and then circle the odd one out: *resentful, bored, angry, maddened, keen, cold, fed up. [Keen.]* If students struggle, write the words on the board for them to copy instead.

Language

T: "*Time crept by like the slugs that slid up the walls of Birt's cave.* What does the writing convey to you?"
[That time feels as if it's passing by very slowly indeed, due to boredom.]

"Comparing one thing to another using the words 'like' or 'as' is known as a *simile*. E.g. 'soar like an eagle', 'brave as a lion'. Comparing one thing to another *without* using the word 'like' or 'as' is known as a *metaphor*, such as 'Time is money' or 'She had stars in her eyes': people are expected not to take them literally."

Ask students to compose one sentence containing a simile and one sentence containing a metaphor.

Fill the Blanks

T writes the "words" below on the board and asks students to fill in the blanks with the appropriate letters – either 'i' 'r' for the /er/ sound (as in dirt) or 'u' 'r' for the /er/ sound (as in turn). They should write 'ir' or 'ur' on their whiteboards and hold them up as the teacher taps each word.

c__l	*[ur]*
t__nip	*[ur]*
sh__t	*[ir]*
sm__k	*[ir]*
h__t	*[ur]*
b__d	*[ir]*
bl__	*[ur]*
f__*	*[ur], [ir]*
l__k	*[ur]*

*Either is correct *(fur, fir)*.

Phoneme Breakdown

(See p16 for instructions.)

Remind students that the suffix 'ed' can be pronounced in three different ways: /d/, /t/ and (two phonemes) /id/.

shirt	*[3*	***sh ir*** *t]*
smirk	*[4*	*s m* ***ir*** *k]*
brazen	*[5*	*b r a* ***ze*** *n]*
sniggered	*[6*	*s n i* ***gg er ed]***

slumped	*[6*	*s l u m p* ***ed]***
tramping	*[7*	*t r a m p i* ***ng]***
panted	*[6*	*p a n t e d]*
howled	*[4*	*h* ***ow*** *l* ***ed]***
wolf	*[4*	*w o l f]*
who	*[2*	***wh*** *o]*

Week 4 Lesson 3: The Troll and his Singing Drum

Reading

i. T reads the first two paragraphs of Story 13 with prosody.
ii. Students quietly read the story in unison with T, placing pointer or finger under each word.
ii. Students read a paragraph each until story is completed.
iv. T provides feedback as necessary.

Recall Quiz

Why don't the girls swim?
[p133 They're afraid of being eaten by a sea-monster.]

Why does Zola return to the lake-shore?
[p134 To retrieve the shell she'd accidentally left behind.]

Why does the troll shove Zola in a drum?
[p135 To create a "magic singing drum".]

Which creatures does Zola's Pa put in the drum?
[p137 Snakes, ants and bees.]

How is Zola welcomed home?
[p138 The girls put on their shell necklaces and dance.]

Phoneme Substitution

hut	*/u/ to /i/*	*[hit]*
rice	*/r/ to /n/*	*[nice]*
tasks	*/t/ to /b/*	*[basks]*
crops	*/c/ to /d/*	*[drops]*
shell	*/sh/ to /b/*	*[bell]*
want	*/a/ to /e/*	*[went]*
down	*/ow/ to /i/*	*[din]*
feeling	*/l/ to /d/*	*[feeding]*

Vocabulary – Positive or Negative

T writes the list below on whiteboard and asks students to copy them down in two columns, the positive ones under "+" and the negative under "-".

cold, smile, shining, hate, sweet, snarl, hum, dance, anger, cry, singing, vile, troll, smirk

*[**Positive:** smile, shining, sweet, hum, dance, singing. **Negative:** cold, snarl, anger, hate, cry, vile, troll, smirk.]*

Vocabulary – Alliteration

T: "There are 26 letters in the English language; 5 of them are vowels (*a, e, i, o, u*) and the rest are consonants – though 'y' sometimes counts as a vowel. Almost every word contains at least one vowel – with exceptions like 'Hmm' and 'Grr!' [Write those on the board.] *Alliteration* is the repetition of the initial consonant sounds of words. This adds music to words and focuses attention on them. Examples include: Mickey Mouse, trick or treat.

"They can sometimes be so hard to pronounce they're known as *tongue-twisters*. One of the most famous is *I sell sea shells on the sea shore*." Ask students to say this line along with you slowly, then repeat slightly faster, then repeat as fast as possible. Repeat the process for *Peter Piper picks a peck of pickled peppers.*

Week 4 Lesson 4: Dog and Jackal

Introducing

/air/ 'are'
/air/ 'air'

Reading

i. **T** reads first part of Story 14 (to p142 penultimate para) with prosody.

ii. Students quietly read the story in unison with T, placing pointer or finger under each word.
iii. Students read a paragraph each until Story 14 is completed.
iv. T provides feedback as necessary.

Comprehension – Oral Questions

Describe the relationship between Dog and Jackal, how and why it changed.
[p141-144 Best friends forever… until the Dog chose the Man and his food and fire over their friendship.]

What is the bargain between Dog and Man?
[p144 To serve humans by hunting and protecting in exchange for food and warmth.]

Comprehension – Oral Discussion

For most of human history survival came before consideration of luxuries like *love.* There's a proverb saying "When poverty comes in through the door, love flies out through the window." Though there's another proverb that "The greatest poverty of all is an absence of love", and a verse in the Bible reading "Better is a dinner of herbs, where love is, than a stalled ox and hatred therewith." Is it reasonable – or at least forgivable – to choose security over friendship?

Phoneme Substitution

bare	*/b/ to /c/*	*[care]*
lair	*/l/ to /f/*	*[fair]*
dare	*/d/ to /sh/*	*[share]*

hare	*/h/ to /f/*	*[fare]*
pair	*/p/ to /h/*	*[hair]*
snare	*/n/ to /t/*	*[stare]*

Vocabulary – Homophones

T repeats the different spellings of the sound /air/ – 'air' and 'are' – demonstrating by writing 'fair' and 'fare' on the whiteboard and explaining their different meanings. Repeat for 'pare' and 'pair' if necessary. T then dictates the following sentences:

He brushed his long blond hair.

She went late to the fair.

The rabbit was not as fast as the hare.

See the pair of twins over there.

That bus fare was not fair!

T checks work immediately, gives feedback and reruns exercise if necessary.

Prosody: Word Emphasis

(See p41 for instructions.)

"**Don't** kill me!" begged the dog.

"Don't **kill** me!" begged the dog.

"Don't kill **me**!" begged the dog.

"Don't kill me!" **begged** the dog.

"Don't kill me!" begged the **dog**.

Week 4 Lesson 5: Consolidation

Recall Quiz

Name three people killed by the Macbeths.
[p109 A brutish terrorist, p113 King Duncan, p115-116 Ban, p119 Macduff's wife and children.]

What happens the third time Birt cries wolf?
[p130 No one believes him or comes to help, so the sheep are killed by the wolf.]

What does the troll do to Zola, and why?
[p135 Shoves her in a drum to sing for him, in order to make lots of money.]

How does the troll die?
[p138 Stung by bees, bitten by red ants and snakes.]

Why does the jackal howl?
[p144 His best friend abandoned him to become the slave of man.]

Phoneme Substitution: Word Chain

T "You will remember the substitution exercises, where one sound was replaced with another to form a new word – e.g. replace the /n/ in 'not' with a /p/ to make 'pot'. I would like you to start off with the word 'sing' – /s/ /i/ /ng/ – and replace any of the sounds with a new sound to form a different word. And to continue until you have ten words written down." Model the first answer on the board, e.g. /s/

can be replaced with /p/ for "ping", *or* /i/ can be replaced with /o/ for "song", *or* /ng/ can be replaced with /n/ for "sin".

Scrambled Sentences

T writes the words below on the board and asks students to rearrange them to make sentences:

anger seemed full he of

rest may fire my by you

you shells pile a of have

rice three and hens piles plump of

up you do and shut are as told

Summarization

T: "A *synopsis* is when a story is condensed into a brief outline of all its important points." Ask students to vote on which of the three stories (*Crying Wolf, The Troll and his Singing Drum, Dog and Jackal*) they want to summarize. Remind them to: a. introduce the characters; b. explain what happened at the start; c. explain how the story develops. Take suggestions for these key points from as many students as possible and write them on the board before whittling them down to circa five bullet-points, as brief and clear as possible and in sequence.

Crossword

(See p35 for instructions.)

*[**Across:** 3. Zola, 4. Jeff, 6. shells*
***Down:** 1. wolf, 2. man, 4. jackal, 5. sheep]*

Across

3. Troll's victim

4. Birt's dad

6. What Zola and pals are collecting

Down

1. What puts Birt out of a job

2. What the dog becomes the slave of

4. Animal howling for his pal the dog

5. What Birt is supposed to take care of

Week 5 Lesson 1: The Face in the Well

Reading

i. Ⓣ reads first two paragraphs of Story 15 with prosody.
ii. Students quietly read the story in unison with T, placing pointer or finger under each word.
ii. Students read one paragraph each until story is complete.
vi. T provides feedback as necessary.

Vocabulary – Oral

Scram, beggar! **Scram** – is it:
a. scam
b. scan
[c. go away]

Pustulated face. **Pustule** – is it:
a. powerful
[b. pimple]
c. remarkable

Repellent virago. **Virago** – is it:
[a. an aggressive woman]
b. a large man
c. an unpleasant child

Sentence Reworking

"The King became set on taking a bride in place of his sweet late wife."
[The monarch was determined to remarry after the loss of his lovely first queen.]

"The woman was well-to-do… but sharp-faced and full of spite."
[The new queen was rich… but nasty-looking and vicious.]

Vocabulary – Positive or Negative

Ⓣ writes the list below on whiteboard, reads each word aloud, students then repeat it in unison whilst holding up their whiteboards with a "+" or "-" sign on to indicate whether the word is a positive or negative one.

spite, pustuled, fair, sharp, unkind, hatred, bold, vile, daring, terror, nice, torment, glee, sad, gladness, thrilled, glared, scoffed, carefree, contempt, horror

*[**Positive:** fair, bold, daring, nice, glee, gladness, thrilled, carefree. **Negative:** sharp, spite, unkind, torment, hatred, vile, sad, glared, scoffed, pustuled, terror, contempt, horror.]*

Characterization

Take answers from as many students as have their hands up.

Think of an adjective to describe the new Queen.
[p147-8, p150, p152-3 Spiteful, sharp, unkind, vicious, smug, mean, snobbish, virago.]

Think of an adjective to describe the King.
[p147-148 Confused, weak, gaslit, manipulated, pathetic.]

Think of an adjective to describe Agnes following her thornbush encounter.
[p151 cut, gashed, scabbed, dishevelled, injured, determined.]

Word Chain

T: "I would like you to start off with the word 'long' - /l/ /o/ /ng/ – and replace any of the sounds with a new sound to form a different word. Continue until you have ten words written down." Model the first answer on the board, e.g. /l/ can be replaced with /s/ for 'song', *or* /o/ can be replaced with /u/ for 'lung', *or* /ng/ can be replaced with /t/ for 'lot'.

Week 5 Lesson 2: Why Spiders Lurk in Corners

Background Knowledge

Spider is Anansi, the African trickster and demi-god, sometimes-man and sometimes-arachnid. The tales of his cunning and selfishness spread with the estimated twelve million Africans enslaved and shipped across the Atlantic in the 16th – 19th centuries. Also known as "Ti Malice" in Haiti and "Aunt Nancy" in the Southern United States.

Introducing

/er/ 'or'

T: "Just as some words spelt with 'u' 'r' have the pronunciation /er/ – like 'turn' – so some words spelt with 'o' 'r' also have this sound – e.g. *worm, worst, worth.* These are almost always words beginning with 'w'."

Reading

i. Students quietly read the first half of the story (until fourth paragraph of p161) in unison with **T**.
ii. T provides feedback as necessary.

Recall Quiz

Name some of the creatures living near Spider.
[p157 Men, children, oxen, cows, pigs, dogs, spiders.]

What does Spider demand his wife does to the ground-nuts before planting them?
[p159 Bake and spice them.]

What does Spider do with the spiced, baked ground-nuts?
[p160 Eats them all.]

Reading

i. Students quietly read the second half of the story (penultimate paragraph of p161 onwards) in unison with **T**.
ii. T provides feedback as necessary.

Vocabulary – Oral

Lamenting his unwillingness to work. **Lament** – is it:
a. celebrate
[b. bemoan]
c. ponder

The sap of the tree seeped. **Sap** – is it:
a. tree bark
b. tree branch
[c. the liquid part of a plant]

Seep – is it:

a. howl

[b. ooze]

c. spurt

What in the world are you blathering about? **Blather** – is it:

a. lie

b. shout

[c. babble]

The shame about to fall on his unwitting wife. **Unwitting** – is it:

a. stupid

b. nice

[c. unaware]

He struck the still, mute form across the face. **Mute** – is it:

[a. silent]

b. mutated

c. unusual

There was nothing for it but to pilfer the nuts he needed! **Pilfer** – is it:

a. to peel

[b. to steal a little at a time]

c. to purchase

Dictation

Shell them and bake them and spice them for me to plant.

When dusk fell, he waved the bag of nuts in his wife's face.

What in the world are you blathering about?

Spider yelled the worst words in the world.

So you are the worthless worm who stole all those nuts!

Characterization

Spider – at first, is he:

[a. nasty and lazy]

b. warm and generous

c. learned and wise

Spider – in the end, is he:

a. smug and content

[b. silent and traumatised]

c. angry and loud

Spider's Wife – is she:

a. confident and outgoing

b. clever and talented

[c. innocent and downtrodden]

Anan – is he:

[a. efficient and furious]

b. happy and optimistic

c. insecure and lazy

Comprehension – Oral Questions

What is Spider's problem at harvest-time? What is his solution?
[p161 Lack of ground-nuts to harvest; stealing someone else's nuts.]

What is Anan's plan to catch the thief?
[p163 Make a rubber man for the thief to get stuck to.]

What are the consequences for all his species of Spider's behaviour?
[p166 They always lurk in the darkest of corners.]

Comprehension – Oral Discussion

Cowed by having a worthless husband who put her down all the time… dismissing her words with a wave of his legs… in the meekest manner… "Nag, nag, nag!" snapped Spider… yelled "Woman! Be off to market!"… worn down by living with Spider for so long… "No wife of mine works on a farm!"… "You nitwit, have you forgotten my words so fast"… the long-suffering woman. Which of these concepts applies to Spider's relationship with his wife: *bullying, gaslighting, coercive control, domestic violence*?

Week 5 Lesson 3: Old Man Legba

Reading

i. Ⓣ reads first paragraph; students echo it back in unison. Repeat until end of story.
ii. T provides feedback as necessary.

Sentence Reworking

"All the blokes, all the dames, *and* all the small fry."
[Every man, woman, and child.]

"Most tribes aren't wised up to me – they just do not have an inkling."
[Most people don't know about me – they just don't have a clue.]

"I go into the sky to report to her all the goings-on, down there on that big globe we made."
[I go to heaven to tell the goddess of the events on planet Earth.]

"She had an all-out yam-fetish."
[The goddess had a total obsession with yams.]

Prosody: Word Emphasis

So you think the Goddess made all things by herself, do you?

So **you** think the Goddess made all things by herself, do you?

So you **think** the Goddess made all things by herself, do you?

So you think the **Goddess** made all things by herself, do you?

So you think the Goddess made **all** things by herself, do you?

So you think the Goddess made all **things** by herself, do you?

So you think the Goddess made all things by **herself**, do you?

So you think the Goddess made all things by herself, **do you?**

Comprehension – Oral Questions

Who created the universe?
[p169-70 the Goddess and Old Man Legba.]

Which tribe hates Legba and why?
[p170 The Fon tribe, because they blame him for everything.]

What has Legba got against the Goddess?
[p171 She cares about yams more than about him. She's happy for him to take the blame for everything that goes wrong.]

How does Legba make the goddess a laughing-stock?
[172-74 By framing her for the theft of her own vegetables.]

Who is suddenly nicer to Legba, and why?
[p174 The Fon tribe, because he is now their only conduit to the Goddess.]

Dictation

Yup – the Goddess gets all the credit, the Goddess's servant gets all the blame.

All the tribes come running, bowing and waving offerings.

They sob and they vow they have no wish for yams.

She compares all the sandals to the sandal-prints in the ground.

I'm telling the Goddess what's what.

Phoneme Breakdown

Warn students that, unlike previous **Phoneme Breakdowns**, this one contains two separated letters that combine to make one sound. For example, 'i' 'e' makes /ie/ as in 'wife'.

goddess	*[5*	*g o **dd** e **ss**]*
bedside	*[6*	*b e d s **i** d **e**]*
zebra	*[5*	*z e b r a]*
print	*[5*	*p r i n t]*
credit	*[6*	*c r e d i t]*
gaze	*[3*	*g **a** z **e**]*
blame	*[4*	*b l **a** m **e**]*
rather	*[4*	*r a **th** **er**]*

Week 5 Lesson 4: The Jaded King

Reading

i. Students quietly read the story in unison with **T**, placing pointer or finger under each word.
ii. T provides feedback as necessary.

Recall Quiz

How many wives does the King have? How many children does the King have?
[p179 Nine and p178 twelve.]

List the suggestions to cheer the King up.
[177-81 Star-gazing, a baby, music, a horse, a jester, dice-games, a bride, stories, clothes, jewellery, food and wine, a contented man's shirt. Take one answer from as many students as possible.]

Which suggestion does the King agree with? What goes wrong?
[p180-181 The shirt off a contented man's back; p182 the fact the contented man isn't wearing a shirt.]

Vocabulary – Oral

Plus umpteen subjects to boss around. **Umpteen** – is it:

a. older teenager
[b. countless]
c. a variety of

He'd cry to his kin. **Kin** – is it:

a. kitten

b. friends

[c. relatives]

Jade for a jaded king. **Jade** – is it:

a. a green gemstone

b. weary

[c. both of the above]

Desolate dames. **Desolate** – is it:

a. a desert

[b. joyless]

c. joyful

Come in, my fine benefactor! **Benefactor** – is it:

[a. a donor]

b. a bonnet

c. a factory worker

Fill the Blanks

T writes the words *palace, emerald, content, white, stars, desolate, mirth* on the board and slowly reads them aloud, asking students to echo each word in unison before conducting a brief discussion of them. Erase the words, replacing them with the sentences below. Ask students to copy out at least three of these lines and fill in the blanks with the words just discussed, without consulting the text. (Note the double length of the underscore for sounds with two letters, and curved lines for split digraphs.)

What do I lack, that I am not _ _ _ _ _ _ _? *[content]*

Gaze up and see the _ _ __ _! *[stars]*

Pure black, fire-red, _ _ _ _ _ _ _-green. *[emerald]*

Dismal blokes and _ _ _ _ _ _ _ _ dames and glum kids. *[desolate]*

No man in the land is as full of _ _ _ as I! *[mirth]*

A pure _ _ _ _ mare to ride. *[white]*

The King strode round his _ _ _ _ _ _. *[palace]*

Vocabulary – Positive or Negative

Ⓣ writes the list below on whiteboard, reads each word aloud, students then repeat the word in unison whilst holding up their whiteboards with a "+" or "-" sign to indicate whether it has a positive or negative meaning.

content, hate, anger, luck, greed, mad, hope, discontented, fun, desperate, blessed, jaded, inspired, happiness, dismal, desolate, smiling, glum, mirth, bliss, grim, scowling, zest, shock

*[**Positive:** content, luck, hope, fun, blessed, inspired, happiness, smiling, mirth, bliss, zest. **Negative:** hate, anger, greed, mad, discontented, desperate, jaded, dismal, desolate, glum, grim, scowling, shock.]*

Graphic Sequencing

Ask the students to draw lines over a double-page spread in their exercise books to divide it thus:

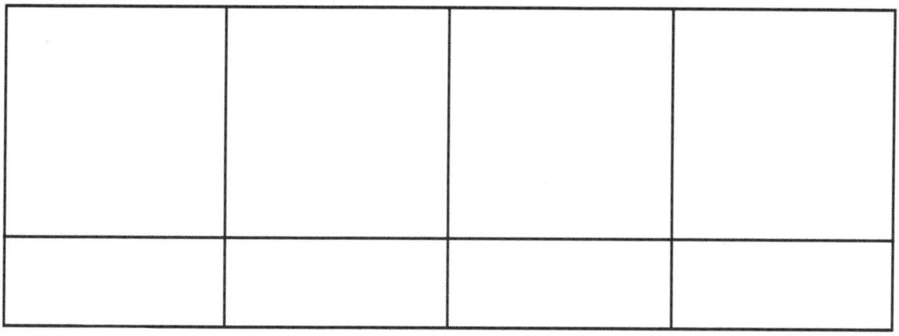

Or thus, depending on the type of exercise book:

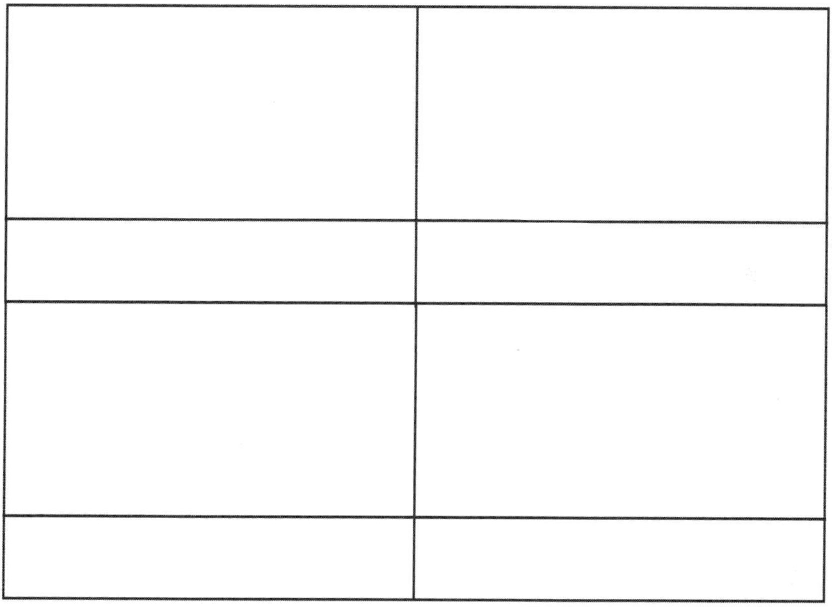

Ask students to pick four scenes from *The Jaded King* or *Old Man Legba* to write or copy a brief sentence about in the lower boxes and illustrate in black and white in the boxes above. Take time and care with this exercise. No need to rush. Sequencing is key.

Week 5 Lesson 5: Consolidation

Recall Quiz for Level 2

How many wives did Henry VIII have?
[p71 Six.]

Which King was obsessed by gold?
[p51 Midas.]

How did Olga and Oleg get their daughter?
[p100 Made her out of snow.]

What went wrong with the Dog-Jackal friendship? Was it ever resolved?
[p144 The dog chose food and warmth over friendship, and the Jackal never got over it.]

How does Macbeth become King?
[p113 By murdering the current incumbent.]

"Crying wolf" is an English idiom. What does it mean, and where does it come from?
[p128-130 It means to call for help when it's not needed, meaning you aren't believed when you are telling the truth and it comes from the Crying Wolf story – originally an Aesop's Fable called The Boy Who Cried Wolf.]

Why does Agnes marry a beggar?
[p152 He cured her smallpox; she gave him her word; possibly, the prophecy somehow compelled her to fulfil it.]

What causes Spider's downfall?

[p157, p161-165 His greed and laziness, which directly led to a very unsuccessful life of crime; Anan's Rubber Man.]

Prefixes

T writes *pre, re, un, sub, dis, mis* on the board. "Prefixes are a group of letters which change the meaning of a word when they are added to the start. Prefixes usually mean a similar thing when they're added to different words. *Pre* (as you can tell from the word 'prefix') usually means 'before': preschool, preheat. *Re* usually means again or back: replay, reappear. *Un* usually means not: unwell, unfair. *Sub* usually means under: subheading, submissive. ***Dis*** and ***mis*** usually have negative meanings: dislike, mistreat."

T writes the left-hand column below on the board, asking students to copy it down and add the correct prefix to each word. Bear in mind that some of these words work with more than one prefix – students should write down all the ones they can think of. Model the first word.

do	*[undo, redo]*
may	*[dismay]*
lock	*[unlock, relock]*
pay	*[prepay, repay]*
way	*[subway]*
fit	*[misfit, unfit, refit]*
obey	*[disobey]*
marine	*[submarine]*
set	*[preset, reset, subset]*

Suffixes

T: "Can anyone remember what a suffix is?" *[A group of letters added to the end of a word that alters its meaning.]*

T writes *ed, ing, ness, less, ful* on the board. Then writes the left-hand column below on the board, asking students to copy it down and add the correct suffix to each word. Bear in mind that some of these words work with more than one suffix – students should write down all the ones they can think of. Model the first word.

bad	*[badness]*
glad	*[gladness]*
end	*[ending, ended, endless]*
shout	*[shouting, shouted]*
worth	*[worthless]*
mad	*[madness]*
bash	*[bashing, bashed, bashful]*
unwilling	*[unwillingness]*
work	*[worked, working]*
life	*[lifeless]*
long	*[longed, longing]*
mind	*[minded, minding, mindless, mindful, mindfulness]*

Characterization

List the names below on the whiteboard. Ask students to create three columns – *Indifferent Selfish Monster* (writing these words on the whiteboard also). Give them ten minutes to place characters in the appropriate column, without looking at the book. Have class discussion afterwards where the answers differ.

King Stork, Rabbit, Dick West, King Midas, King Log, Scorpion, Hal Rex, Nate, Oleg & Olga, Macbeth, Dame Macbeth, Dog [from Dog and Jackal not Ice Lass], Birt, Troll, Agnes, Clare's Father, Spider, Legba, Jaded King, Rane

*[**King Stork** – monster, **Rabbit** – selfish, **Dick West** – selfish, **King Midas** – selfish, **King Log** – indifferent, **Scorpion** – monster, **Hal Rex** – monster, **Nate** – selfish, **Oleg & Olga** – selfish, **Macbeth** – monster, **Dame Macbeth** – monster, **Dog** – selfish, **Birt** – selfish, **Troll** – monster, **Agnes** – selfish, **Clare's Father** – indifferent, **Spider** – selfish, **Legba** – none of the above, **Jaded King** – selfish, **Rane** – selfish. Obviously there is room for debate, e.g. the Scorpion couldn't help himself, Agnes's initial levels of bullying may qualify her for "monster", Dick had every right to be upset, etc.]*

Crossword for Level 2

*[**Across:** 3. log, 4. Legba, 6. gold, 8. Macduff, 9. shirt, 10. Scorpion*
***Down:** 1. Kate, 2. Zola, 5. groundnuts, 7. hanging, 9. Stork, 11. Rabbit]*

Mastery Assessments

T to arrange for individual Level 2 Mastery Assessments.

Across

3. The Frog's first King

4. Servant who helped the Goddess make the world

6. What King Midas obsesses about

8. Slayer of Macbeth

9. What the Jaded King needed to make him content

10. Killer of Sog the Frog

Down

1. Name of three of Hal Rex's wives

2. Victim of a troll

5. Downfall of Spider

7. How Nate perished

9. The Frog's second King

11. She who thinks she has lots of pals

Level 2 Word Lists

All words should be encoded via the sound-through-the-word protocol, with students whispering each sound as they write. Words containing unusual GPCs, or not wholly decodable at this stage, are flagged up in boxes. See **Introduction** p7-8 and **Appendix D: Spelling & Dictation** p136-139.

NB: Single-syllable Basic Alphabetic Code words are not included in the spelling lists.

Level 2: Poem 1: I am Cat: Playing With the Rat

Introducing: suffix 'ing'

One-Syllable Advanced Code	**Multi-Syllable Basic + Advanced Code**
sleek	grinning
	hinting
	playing
	preening

Level 2 Story 1: The Frogs Demand a King

Introducing: grapheme 'ng', sound /ng/

Please note that if a word has a short vowel, its last letter is usually doubled when adding an 'ing' (e.g. beg → begging). This is not the case when a word has a long vowel (e.g. pray → praying).

Please see https://www.youtube.com/watch?v=thyoodo5-V0 for a more comprehensive exploration of this 'rule'.

One-Syllable

Advanced Code

sheep
stork
long
king

Multi-Syllable

Basic + Advanced Code

begging
bragging
blessing
grabbing
jumping
howling
bowing
swimming
swinging
fleeing
bleeding
nagging
pecking
nothing
splashing
napping
snapping
praying
hopping
demanding
ignorant

Level 2 Story 2: She Who Has Lots of Pals…

One-Syllable

Advanced Code

shy
short
snort
horn
hound

Multi-Syllable

Basic + Advanced Code

slavering
moral
support
bitter
better
bluster
stagger
elder
scamper

trembling	number
drumming	sweetest
panting	contempt
hunting	another
braying	assassin
bounding	reprimand
terror	devilish
horror	buttercup

Level 2 Story 3: The Fox and the Robin

One-Syllable Advanced Code	Multi-Syllable Basic + Advanced Code
small	robin
tweet	belong
loud	thinking
	spitting
	dropping

Level 2 Poem 2: I am Cat: Playing in the Tree

One-Syllable Advanced Code	Multi-Syllable Basic + Advanced Code
–	running
	peeping
	sitting
	slipping

Level 2 Story 4: Keep the Cat

Introducing: grapheme 'ey', sound /ae/, suffix 'ed'

One-Syllable Advanced Code

they
hey
prey
wheel
said
some

Multi-Syllable Basic + Advanced Code

digging
swigging
pelting
licking
obey
survey
yesterday
ruffian

Level 2 Story 5: Sad Slim and Spitting Freda

One-Syllable Advanced Code

steep

Multi-Syllable Basic + Advanced Code

within
behind
jogging
spinning
springing
huffing
puffing
creeping
dashing
stamping
stomping
slithering

Level 2 Story 6: King Midas

One-Syllable
Advanced Code
why

Multi-Syllable
Basic + Advanced Code
buzzing
doing
glittering
yapping
fizzing
shimmering
hankering

Level 2 Story 7: Scorpion and Frog

One-Syllable
Advanced Code
zing
pout
drown

Multi-Syllable
Basic + Advanced Code
utter
mutter
nutter
ponder
monster
desert
toxic
perish
horrid
peckish
madman
kidding
stinging
blinking
nibbling
helping
clinging
paddling
scuttling
sinking
tempting
depressing
malignant
scorpion
sadistic
whenever

Level 2 Story 8: Smug Rane and Zog the Frog

Introducing: split digraph 'a-e', sound /ae/, split digraph 'i-e', sound /ie/

One-Syllable Code

life
wife
lime
time
dive
five
like
fine
mime
wise
rise
bite
side
hide
bride
smile
pale
daze
make
take
lake
late
tame
shame
game

Multi-SyllableAdvanced Basic + Advanced Code

frowning
setting
dripping
singing
tossing
kissing
thanking
fortress

Level 2 Story 9: Hal Rex

One-Syllable Advanced Code

three
fleet
sheet
clown
ripe
nine
wine
pile
ride
dame
came
axe
save
rave
grave
brave
wake
tale

Multi-Syllable Basic + Advanced Code

female
bucket
about
mistress
arrogant
ever
hanging
patting
getting
holding
limping
calling
stinking
wedding
sobbing

Level 2 Story 10: Hanging Nate

Introducing: split digraph 'o-e', sound /oe/, grapheme 'ore', sound /or/

One-Syllable
Advanced Code

cloud
trout
lout
deed
made
hate
fate
date
safe
name
fame
lame
blame
blaze
wave
nose
smoke
froze
home
swore
snore
bore
mole
hole
stole
spoke
more
fray
fang
gown

Multi-Syllable
Basic + Advanced Code

minstrel
waver
plunder
betray
astray
adore
before
intend
silent
pocket
sixteen
witness
fondness
smallpox
Scotland
pirate
bishop
despot
banging
rubbing

dote
poke
joke
broke
lord
pork
wide
tide
fire
slime
crime
swine
clay

scrubbing
finding
fishing
feeding
feeling
weeping
keeping
spending
hitting
slapping
tracking
attempting

Level 2 Poem 3: Space Race

Introducing: grapheme 'ze', sound /z/, grapheme 'ce', sound /s/

One-Syllable
Advanced Code
lope
mope
globe
ice
price
pine
slide
breeze
freeze
steel
glance
space
place

Multi-Syllable
Basic + Advanced Code
orbit
rocket
endless

Level 2 Story 11: Ice Lass

Introducing: split digraph 'u-e', sound /oo/

One-Syllable Advanced Code

mice
strike
dine
stroke
scale
same
snake
cute
tune
mule
rule
stroll
dance
tore
love
pure

Multi-Syllable Basic + Advanced Code

expose
stubborn
panther
massive
sheepskin
offspring
clapping
sculpting
slinking
drinking
dragging
refreshing
beginning
outlandish

Level 2 Play 1: Macbeth

Introducing: grapheme 'ur', sound /er/, grapheme 'ar', sound /ar/ grapheme 'gh', sound /g/, grapheme 'ere', sound /air/

One-Syllable Advanced Code

gaze
fake
torn
born
gore

return
disturb
murder
absurd
hurray

outburst
note
curse
hurt
dire
vile
thing
ghost
dark
hard
start
prince

Multi-Syllable
Basic + Advanced Code
cannot
power
anger
celebrate
murmur
welcome
overcome
dagger
embrace
graveyard
hero
shaking
taking
bursting
greeting
strutting
stabbing
terrorist
remember

Level 2 Story 12: Crying Wolf

Introducing: grapheme 'ir', sound /er/, grapheme 'o', sound /u/
grapheme 'o', sound /00/

One-Syllable
Advanced Code
dirt
shirt
smirk
nice
wolf
storm
white
vale

Multi-Syllable
Basic + Advanced Code
snigger
upset
dullness
asking
gazing
tramping
putting
humming
shining
crying

Level 2 Story 13: The Troll and his Singing Drum

One-Syllable
Advanced Code

shore
lurk
ale
girl
snarl

Multi-Syllable
Basic + Advanced Code

replace
necklace
woman
marvel
sweeping
outing
giving
biting
jeering
morning
crashing
falling
refreshment
amazement
Africa
everlasting

Level 2 Story 14: Dog and Jackal

Introducing: grapheme 'are', sound /air/, grapheme 'air', sound /air/

One-Syllable
Advanced Code

dare
snare
hare
stare
glare
bare
spare
starve
flame
share
shake
slave
gale
bone
lone
air

hair
lair
fair
curl
Multi-Syllable
Basic + Advanced Code
declare
endure
lying
dying
daring
having
shivering
evening
together

Level 2 Story 15: The Face in the Well

One-Syllable
Advanced Code
hope
thorn
sharp
care
mare
grace
glimpse
price
spite
sure
Multi-Syllable
Basic + Advanced Code
prepare
fixate
relate
funeral
hatred
torment
consent
huntsmen
farewell
farmland
carefree
repent
pustule
totter
palace
beggar
blocking
repellent
virago

Level 2 Story 16: Why Spiders Lurk in Corners

Introducing: grapheme 'or', sound /er/

One-Syllable Advanced Code	Multi-Syllable Basic + Advanced Code
fade	midday
laze	dismiss
pull	workmen
meek	harvest
spade	rubber
tuck	slander
mute	pilfer
spice	sunset
smart	cunning
worn	ignore
worth	innocent
worm	optimistic
word	suffering
world	

Level 2 Story 17: Old Man Legba

One-Syllable Advanced Code	Multi-Syllable Basic + Advanced Code
tribe	report
star	goddess
	garden
	zebra
	mistake
	scoundrel
	beloved

Level 2 Story 18: The Jaded King

One-Syllable

Advanced Code

throne
twelve
jade
robe
mirth
perk
pipe

Multi-Syllable

Basic + Advanced Code

spirit
darling
princess
umpteen
despond
jester
sunrise
inspire
smelling
turning
contentment
emerald
abundant
desolate
benefactor

Appendices

Appendix A: Fluency & Prosody

Fluency

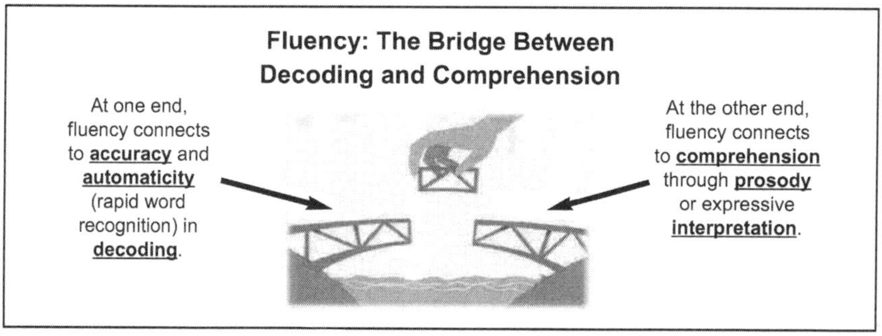
Fluency: The Bridge Between
Decoding and Comprehension
At one end, fluency connects to accuracy and automaticity (rapid word recognition) in decoding.
At the other end, fluency connects to comprehension through prosody or expressive interpretation.

"An estimated 20% of children leave primary phase each year unable to decode with sufficient fluency to read the kinds of texts they will encounter at secondary school. Essentially, the more slowly you read, the more working memory capacity is taken up by decoding, leaving fewer cognitive resources available for comprehension. If children cannot decode fluently then it follows they would be unable to understand a written text even if they could understand the same information given verbally!"

– David Didau,

https://learningspy.co.uk/featured/why-just-reading-might-make-more-of-a-difference-than-teaching-reading/

"Fluent readers have honed three key skills which can be practised regularly in the classroom: accuracy, speed and

prosody. They are also skills which can be improved when practised repeatedly and transferred from one text to another. More so than reading skills (e.g. inference, prediction, summary) which are highly dependent on prior knowledge."
https://www.manicstreetteachers.com/post/focus-on-fluency

"Fluency is the ability to read with Expression, Automatic word recognition, Rhythm and phrasing, and Smoothness (EARS). Fluency has traditionally been neglected in reading programs (Allington, 1983), and when it has been embraced, it is often misunderstood (Rasinski, 2006, 2012). So having a good grasp of reading fluency is certainly an appropriate place to start. We often think of the act of reading as involving two major competencies: word decoding (phonics) and comprehension. Fluency is, in a sense, a critical link between those two competencies (Rasinski, 2010)."
http://teacher.scholastic.com/education/pdfs/Megabook-Intro.pdf

"There is a substantial body of evidence to suggest that repeated oral reading of short texts that are towards the upper limits of children's current reading ability can support children's development of the components of fluency, which are essential to reading comprehension… it should never be dissociated from the ultimate purpose of reading, and well-chosen texts should ensure that the comprehension undertaken during fluency practice is valuable on its own terms."
– Christopher Such,
https://primarycolour.home.blog/2020/07/12/five-ways-to-ensure-that-your-teaching-of-reading-is-effective/#_edn1

"Fluent reading supports comprehension because pupils' cognitive resources are freed from focusing on word recognition and can be redirected towards comprehending the text. This can be developed through: guided oral reading instruction – teachers model fluent reading of a text, then pupils read the same text aloud with appropriate feedback.

Repeated reading – pupils reread a short and meaningful passage a set number of times or until they reach a suitable level of fluency. It is important to understand pupils' current capabilities and teach accordingly. Most pupils will need an emphasis on developing reading fluency, but some pupils may need a focus on more basic skills, such as decoding and phonological awareness."

https://educationendowmentfoundation.org.uk/

Prosody

"Fluent decoders also need teachers to model reading with prosody – that is to say, reading with the 'music' of the text in mind – the changes in pace, in tone and the way we stress different words in sentences, all of which add meaning to the words on the page. Some children don't realise that this is how their reading in their head is meant to sound to them!"
– Clare Sealy, Head of Education Improvement, States of Guernsey

Engaging account of prosody and its importance. Paula J. Schwanenflugel, Nancy Flanagan
https://www.psychologytoday.com/gb/blog/reading-minds/201701/the-music-reading-aloud

Comprehensive guide incorporating accuracy, automaticity, comprehension and prosody. Martin Galway, Herts for Learning
https://www.hertsforlearning.co.uk/blog/a-field-guide-to-reading-fluency

Appendix B: Comprehension & Inference

Comprehension

"Comprehension can neither be expected to develop on its own, nor can it be taught in isolation from the many aspects of language and human culture that impinge upon our reading experience."
– Dianne Murphy,
https://thinkingreadingwritings.wpcomstaging.com/2016/10/27/seven-steps-to-improving-reading-comprehension/

"Three factors are important in reading comprehension: monitoring your comprehension, relating the sentences to one another, and relating the sentences to things you already know."
– Daniel Willingham, 'The Usefulness of *Brief* Instruction in Reading Comprehension Strategies',
https://www.aft.org/sites/default/files/periodicals/CogSci.pdf

"Students progress at a much faster rate in phonics when the bulk of instructional time is spent on applying the skills to authentic reading and writing experiences, rather than isolated skill-and-drill work."
– Wiley Blevins, ILA Literacy, 'Leadership Brief: Meeting the Challenges of Early Literacy Phonics Instruction',
https://www.literacyworldwide.org/

"Not only must a reader be capable of orthographic mapping and self-teaching if he is to eventually acquire a sight-vocabulary of 60,000 or more words, he must also be an *avid* reader – someone who joyfully and willingly reads across multiple genres and subject areas whenever he gets the chance. A child will read in this manner only if a competent teacher

provided him with the skills he needs to do so."
– Stephen Parker,
https://www.parkerphonics.com

"Teaching kids to monitor their comprehension and if they are not understanding a text to take charge and try to fix it; teaching kids to read text and to stop occasionally to sum up for themselves what the text is telling them (and to go back if they aren't getting it); teaching kids to ask themselves questions about what they are reading and to go back and reread if they can't answer those questions (kind of a discussion in the head); teaching them to look for a text's structure to figure out what the parts are and how they fit together (story mapping is the most common example of this support). There are some others but those are the ones with the most research support and the biggest payoff. (And, teaching kids more than one strategy makes a lot of sense too – apparently different strategies help students to solve different problems, so having multiple strategies is beneficial.)"
– Tim Shanahan,
https://www.shanahanonliteracy.com/

"Reading comprehension is a notoriously complex and knotty construct. It is influenced by multiple sources of variation at the level of text, activity and purpose for reading, as well as by individual skills related to knowledge of the linguistic system, general knowledge and word-level processes. Within this complex picture, vocabulary knowledge is recognised as the lynchpin of reading comprehension, the 'central connection point between the word identification system and the comprehension system.'"
– Perfetti & Stafura,
https://www.eminamclean.com/post/explicit-vocabulary-instruction-across-grades-and-subjects

Knowledge is required for comprehension: What is the subject of this passage?

"This process can take anywhere from about one hour to all day. The length of time depends on the elaborateness of the final product. Only one substance is necessary for this process. However, the substance must be quite abundant and of suitable consistency. The substance is best used when it is fresh, as its lifespan can vary. Its lifespan varies depending on where the substance is located. If one waits too long before using it, the substance may disappear. This process is such that almost anyone can do it. The easiest method is to compress the substance into a denser mass than it had in its original state. This process gives a previously amorphous substance some structure. Other substances can be introduced near the end of the process to add to the complexity of the final product. These substances are not necessary. However, many people find that they add to the desired effect. At the end of the process, the substance is usually in a pleasing form.

"Now read the text again, but with the title 'Building a Snowman.' Feel different? This is the difference that makes. This is what happens when a link is missing."
– Solomon Kingsnorth, 'Building a Snowman', *Understanding and Teaching Reading Comprehension*, Jan Oakhill et al, Routledge, 2014,
https://medium.com/solomonkingsnorth/reading-comprehension-a-new-approach-570d39ffac79

Inference

"The first thing we need to teach children about inference is their own crucial role in checking they are understanding what the text is saying as they read. The book isn't going to stop and repeat itself or explain in more detail if they don't understand. Successful readers expect to understand what they read and know what to do when they spot themselves not understanding. We need to explicitly teach children to check

that what they are reading makes sense to them; to nod along as they read in the same way we nod along when someone is talking to us. If something doesn't make sense they should say 'huh?' to themselves and stop and reread the last sentence or two more slowly, to see if that helps. If someone was speaking, we'd ask them to repeat what they had said. Unfortunately, a book can't rephrase what is written, but if we reread, we might find the bit that is tricky and then be able to make more sense of it... The inference problem is really a knowledge problem."
– Clare Sealey,
https://primarytimery.com/2017/05/01/infernal-inference/

"While many teachers would ask questions and point out contextual clues that would help to infer an unknown word as part of teaching a text, there is little to be gained from teaching it as a strategy or a skill. The pupils who are picking up on this, do so without much teaching and those who aren't lack knowledge."
– Tarjinder Gill,
http://www.teach-well.com/reading-strands-are-meaningless/

Appendix C: Basic Grammar

Verbs

Action verbs express what is happening (do, work). State verbs express a situation (be, have).

Nouns

Nouns represent people (teacher, Mary), places (town, Asia) and things (table, music).

Adjectives

An adjective is a word that tells us more about a noun (big, red, expensive).

Adverbs

Adverbs tell us more about verbs, adjectives or adverbs (loudly, really, extremely).

Determiners

Determiners limit or determine a noun (the, an, two, some).

Prepositions

A preposition expresses the relationship of a noun or pronoun to another word (at, in, from).

Pronouns

Pronouns are small words like you, ours, some, that can take the place of a noun.

Conjunctions

Conjunctions join two parts of a sentence (and, but, though).

Interjections

Short exclamations with no real grammatical value (ah, dear, er).
https://www.englishclub.com/grammar/parts-of-speech.htm

Morphology

Approximately 90% of 2-syllable+ words have Greek and Latin roots – see also: *The Art & Science of Teaching Primary Reading*, Christopher Such, Sage Publications, 2021: Appendix B, 'Latin and Greek Root Words for Primary Schools'.

Ten common prefixes:

- anti- against. antifreeze.
- bio- life. biology.
- dis- not, opposite of. disagree.
- en-, em- cause to. encode, embrace.
- fore- before. forecast.
- in-, im-, il-, ir- not. injustice, impossible.
- inter- between. interact
- re- again. reaction.
- trans- across. transport.
- un- not. unfair.

http://ieapng.net/curriculum/english/docs/language/Prefix_Suffix.pdf

Word Roots

Jason Wade quoting John Ayto, *Dictionary of Word Origins*: *"The underlying meaning of etymology is 'finding the underlying or true meaning of words'".*
https://jweducation.co.uk/2021/04/13/rootrepository/

Appendix D: Spelling & Dictation

Spelling

"A study of over 17,000 English words, found that, with a knowledge of the main phoneme-grapheme spelling patterns, 96% of words have entirely predictable spellings and only 4% (or less) are 'true oddities'."
– Hanna, Hanna, Hodges, and Rudorf, 1966

Word Lists: Introduction

Single-syllable Basic Alphabetic Code words are not included in the spelling lists. However, the Multi-Syllable word lists do include a number of multi-syllable Basic Code words (e.g. wisdom) as well as Advanced Code ones (e.g. dismay).

All words should be encoded via the sound-through-the-word protocol, with students whispering each sound as they write. Words containing unusual GPCs, or not wholly decodable at this stage, are flagged up in boxes.

When dictating words:

- Focus on the 'tricky' spelling of words with unusual GPCs, e.g. 'wh**a**t'.
- Clearly emphasize the 'tricky' element using a 'spelling' voice, e.g. 'mod**el**'.
- Clearly emphasize the unstressed sound in multi-syllable words, e.g. 'an/i/**mal**'.
- Remind students that each chunk usually contains a vowel sound.

- Remind students that a single sound – e.g. /ll/ in 'intellect' – must not be split between chunks: in/tell/ect, never in/tel/lect.

Simple Ways to Use the Word Lists

- Select a few words from the story your students are studying and ask them carefully to write each word, remembering to whisper each sound as they write.
- Ask students to select examples of one sound with different spellings – e.g. sound /ee/, spellings 'e' and 'ee' ('tree' and 'be' from Story 1), or sound /ie/, spellings 'i' and 'y' ('my' and 'find' from Stories 6 and 8), instructing them to write down as many examples as possible and underline the target sound.
- Select twenty words at random from recent stories' Word Lists, write them on the board and invite students to compose a sentence using at least three of the words. With more advanced students, ask for a short paragraph.
- Syllable chunking of 2- and 3-syllable words.
- Select boxed words for writing sound by sound.

Syllable Chunking Practice

Each chunk normally contains one vowel

1 syllable gr**ee**n

2 syllables w**i**s/d**o**m

3 syllables **e**l/**e**/g**a**nt

T invites students to draw three lines on their whiteboards and models the word "el/e/gant", with a pause between syllables and with an exaggerated dropping-of-jaw movement, placing hand under chin to emphasise each vowel sound. T then reads a series of words from the **Word Lists**. Students write one syllable per line, whispering each sound, before holding up their whiteboards on the pre-arranged signal. T promptly corrects any errors that arise. Students erase their answers. T carefully articulates the next word.

Drop, Swop and Double 'Rule' Demonstrated by Sue Lloyd, Jolly Phonics
https://tcrw.co.uk/materials-linked-to-phonic-knowledge/vowels-how-they-work/part-4-drop-swop-and-double/

Words with Unusual Spellings

"Support children to focus on the part of the word that is 'tricky', ensuring that the other sound-spelling correspondences are correct. For example, when spelling the word 'float' students can be fairly confident about the graphemes require to represent the /f/, /l/ and /t/ phonemes; this ensures that they can concentrate their mind on the remaining 'oa' grapheme, which also helps teachers to focus their assistance on just a portion of a word." – Jennifer Chew, OBE.

Schwa

There are numerous words where an unstressed syllable contains a vowel that sounds more like a soft, weak /u/ than its actual phoneme. E.g. banana, balloon, problem, family, bottom, etc. When dictating words with these schwas, clearly emphasise the sounds of the actual letters rather than the way they are usually pronounced: /b/ /o/ /tt/ **/o/** /m/ not /b/ /o/ /tt/ /u/ /m/.

https://www.readingrockets.org/article/two-four-syllable-words-short-vowels-and-schwa

https://keystoliteracy.com/blog/teaching-the-schwa-sound-in-unaccented-syllables/

Dictation

a. Teacher dictates the whole sentence.
b. Students repeat the sentence.
c. Teacher dictates the first part of the sentence.
d. Students repeat the first part of the sentence.
e. Students write the first part of the sentence.
f. Teacher circulates and provides feedback.
g. Teacher dictates the second part of the sentence.
h. Students repeat the second part of the sentence.
i. Students write the second part of the sentence.
– Anita L. Archer, Spelling Sentence Dictation

See also **MRI Tutor Guide**.

Appendix E: Recommended Reading

Books

Christopher Such, *The Art and Science of Teaching Primary Reading,* Sage Publications, 2021

Lyn Stone, *Reading For Life*, David Fulton, 2019

David Didau, *Making Meaning in English*, Routledge, 2021

Alex Quigley, *Closing the Vocabulary Gap*, Routledge, 2018

Beck, McKeown, Kucan, *Bringing Words to Life*, Second Edition, Guilford Press, 2013

Hochman and Wexler, *The Writing Revolution*, Josey Bass, 2017

Klingner, Vaughn, Boardman, *Teaching Reading Comprehension to Students with Learning Difficulties*, Second Edition, Guilford Press, 2015

Tom Sherrington, *Rosenshine's Principles in Action*, John Catt, 2019

Daniel T. Willingham, *Why Don't Students Like School*, Josey Bass, 2021 (2nd edition)

Christopher Curtis, *Develop Brilliant Reading*, Collins, 2022 Collection of readymade and photocopiable reading tests to spot problem areas and direct teaching (KS3).

Kate Jones, *Retrieval Practice: Primary*, John Catt, 2022 Practical guide, also useful for tutors of mature learners.

Jo Facer, *Simplicity Rules*, Routledge, 2019

Natalie Wexler, *The Knowledge Gap*, Penguin Random House, 2019

Ann Sullivan, *A Parent's Guide to Phonics*, phonicsforpupilswith specialeducationalneeds.com

Lauren Meadows, *Pupil Book Study: Reading*, John Catt, 2022

Greg Ashman, *Cognitive Load Theory*, Corwin, 2022

Articles and Blogs

Reading in secondary schools and supporting weaker readers, Gill Jones, Deputy Director, Schools and Early Education
https://educationinspection.blog.gov.uk/2022/04/28/supporting-secondary-school-pupils-who-are-behind-with-reading/

Eminently readable history of reading instruction (NB: there are slight differences between US and UK approach – mainly the delayed introduction of letter names in the UK), Stephen Parker
https://www.parkerphonics.com/post/a-brief-history-of-reading-instruction

Research-based strategies all teachers should know, Barak Rosenshine
https://www.aft.org/sites/default/files/periodicals/Rosenshine.pdf

Seminal article on memory, Daniel Willingham
https://www.aft.org/sites/default/files/periodicals/willingham_0.pdf

Succinct explanation of questioning routines, Tom Sherrington
https://teacherhead.com/2022/04/18/the-dynamics of questioning-agile-responsive-nimble-purposeful/

Practical ways to scaffold classroom dialogue, Tom Sherrington
https://teacherhead.com/2021/12/01/five-ways-to-scaffold-classroom-dialogue/

Survey of evidence-informed teaching, Tom Sherrington
https://teacherhead.com/2021/07/19/what-does-it-mean-to-be-evidence-informed-in-teaching/

Addressing underachieving groups, Tom Sherrington
https://teacherhead.com/2018/09/17/to-address-underachieving-groups-teach-everyone-better/

Cold calling, Tom Sherrington
https://teacherhead.com/2022/02/06/cold-call-forensics-purpose-spirit-details/

Power of comparison, Andy Tharby
https://reflectingenglish.wordpress.com/2015/09/27/the-power-of-comparison/

Micro-moves for academic talk, Alex Quigley
https://www.theconfidentteacher.com/2022/04/6-micro-moves-for-academic-talk/

Importance of oracy, Mary Myatt
https://www.marymyatt.com/blog/walking-the-talk

Teaching spelling 'Dos and Don'ts', Monique Nowers
https://howtoteachreading.org.uk/the-dos-and-donts-of-teaching-spelling/

Early reading acquisition for secondary teachers, Neil Almond
https://nutsaboutteaching.wordpress.com/2021/03/08/ramble16-what-should-every-secondary-school-teacher-should-know-about-early-reading

Building automaticity into handwriting, Sarah Barker
https://roundlearning.org/2016/11/19/

Handwriting – the Tucha Experiments, Sarah Barker
https://roundlearning.org/2018/12/09/

Tier two vocabulary for primary teachers (also applicable for older students), Christopher Such
https://primarycolour.home.blog/2019/06/14/tier-two-vocabulary-for-primary-teachers-the-3-4-5-list/

Advice on involving all students in thinking and providing a good sample of responses, Tom Sherrington
https://teacherhead.com/2022/08/20/the-six-most-common-topics-in-my-teacher-coaching-and-cpd

One-stop shop for Tom Sherrington's *Five Ways To* series, with one-page summaries by David Goodwin
https://teacherhead.com/2022/07/01/five-ways-to-the-collection/

Resetting our understanding of forgetting, Evidence for Educators
https://www.manicstreetteachers.com/post/stop-screaming-at-similes-like-a-banshee

Advice on redrafting, Chris Curtis
https://learningfrommymistakesenglish.blogspot.com/2022/09/one-word-drafting.html?spref=tw

Figurative language making for a richer experience, Manic Street Teachers
https://www.manicstreetteachers.com/post/stop-screaming-at-similes-like-a-banshee

Leading Reading Interventions at KS3, Jasmine Lane, ResearchED Sept 22
https://docs.google.com/presentation/d/1dNjGUNUVAeEf0eZd3sVawervkmoiZ0gPKI_K_bNRsCg/edit#slide=id.p

Videos

Short demonstration of reading visualisation, Mr H
https://www.youtube.com/watch?v=g2qTCMprE2w&list=PL4BRzbvGE5G5JmQFfwib4r9MkNwlCaw3q

Reading development in under 8 minutes, Tips for Teachers, Christopher Such interviewed by Craig Barton
https://youtu.be/03XZFaQyqJU

Damaging effects of illiteracy, Dr Steven Dykstra
https://www.literacypodcast.com/podcast-episodes/episode/794c0450/ep-100-trauma-and-reading-with-dr-steven-dykstra

Orthographic mapping, Lyn Stone
https://www.youtube.com/watch?v=KluwKnZqJEQ

Overview of Rosenshine's Principles in Action
https://catalyst.cg.catholic.edu.au/resources/an-introduction-to-rosenshines-10-principles-of-instruction-tom-sherrington/

Orthographic Mapping: What It Is and Why It's So Important, The Reading League
https://www.youtube.com/watch?v=XfRHcUeGohc

Appendix F: Glossary

Alphabetic Code: relationship between sounds (phonemes) and the letters that symbolize these sounds (graphemes).

Echo Reading: rereading strategy designed to help students develop expressive, fluent reading with T first reading a sentence, or short paragraph, followed by students echoing it.

Fluency: reading with accuracy, automaticity and prosody.

Grapheme: written representation of a single sound (phoneme).

GPC: Grapheme-Phoneme Correspondence; link between a sound and its letter(s).

Homographs: words with the same spelling but with a different meaning (e.g. fair (blond/honest)).

Homophones: words sounding exactly the same but with different spellings/meanings (e.g. bear, bare).

Morphology: study of the parts of a word (morphemes) that cannot be subdivided further.

Orthographic mapping: process whereby the sound/letter(s) of each word is fixed in memory. This results in the words being read without conscious decoding.

Phoneme: smallest unit of sound in a word that is distinguishable.

Prefix: letter or group of letters placed at the start of a word that changes the word's meaning (e.g. historic – prehistoric).

Prosody: reflecting the sounds of natural spoken language including rhythm, stress, intonation and flow.

Suffix: letter or letters added at the end of a word to make a new word, generally changing its word class from either noun or verb to adjective or adverb (e.g. child→childish, sad→sadly).

Synthetic Phonics: teaching of reading via the incremental introduction and thorough practice of the sounds of the English Alphabetic Code.

Published in the UK by Piper Books Ltd, 13 Southfield Road,
Oxford OX4 1NX

Visit us online at www.piperbooks.co.uk

Scan to discover more

MRI: Mature Reading Instruction Programme:

MRI Level 1

11 stories and plays

MRI Level 2

22 stories, plays and poems

MRI Level 3

12 stories and plays

MRI Level 4A

10 stories, plays and poems

MRI Level 4B

9 stories and plays

MRI Level 5A

5 stories and plays

MRI Level 5B

12 stories, plays and poems

MRI Tutor Guide

The photocopiable MRI Tutor Guide enables all teachers to assess exactly where a student is in their progress towards becoming a competent reader. Information and procedures are clearly and simply explained.

Contents include:

Practical Teaching Points, Initial and Final Assessments, Background Information About the Stories, Record Keeping, Fluency Practice, Copying and Dictation Exercises, Frequently Asked Questions, and Troubleshooting.

Printed in Great Britain
by Amazon

30700505R00082